MW01248421

More
Reflections
and Such,
in the Key of
Life

Mobe McScrotom

authorHOUSE®

AuthorHouse™
1663 Liberty Drive
Bloomington, IN 47403
www.authorhouse.com
Phone: 1 (800) 839-8640

Published by AuthorHouse 07/17/2019

ISBN: 978-1-5462-2094-7 (sc)
ISBN: 978-1-5462-2093-0 (hc)

Library of Congress Control Number: 2017918904

Cover Art by E.K. Werntz

Thanks to M. Koelzer for her consideration and input.

Print information available on the last page.

This book is printed on acid-free paper.

A Dedication:

To Melanie,

For her love and her strength.

Daughter, sister, wife, and mother.

Teacher and warrior, in the truest sense.

We will not forget . . .

See you soon.

Be blessed.

Love is Love
    For whatever it is
That you feel it
    And you know it is enough
As sure as a dog is
    God coming at you backwards
Sometime it is terribly tough
    To do what you have to do
Even when your heart and your spirit know
    Sometime you have to love them to the point
To set them free
    To let them go ...

Living is like walking through
   A thousand different rooms
Leaving pictures on the walls
   Of friends and places
Framed memories of everything
   One has experienced on their journey
The Good — the Bad — the Ugly
   All the joys and disgraces
In this bit of time between eternities ...

We are given these few moments here
   To discern and learn of the Truth
The Infinite Wisdom of the Ages
   The Book is open for all to see
But you have to read the pages ...

Instant in resentment
    With some bitter animosities
Self-respect intermingled with
    Respect for the foe
Antique in courtesy
    A true warrior hostility
Always in search to learn
    What is not yet known ...

Magnanimous to forgive
    The instant reparation made
No littleness
    No variant in form
Exception — Contempt is mixed with hatred
    Then no words can convey
Any sense of the sheer intensity
    Of the scorn
That lays in wait
    Contemplate
Push on ...

You have to go deep down to

The depths of your soul

Then develop your "eye" to see it

There is an inherent beauty to everything

And your spirit needs badly

To feel it ...

And time marches on.

A coup d'état of emotion
　　Humanity being washed away
By the virtual storm of technology
　　That encircles mankind everyday

It is not about the truth any longer
　　Just the "Quality of Stagecraft" of the lie
Pseudo events now taken for reality
　　And no one cares at all or wants to know why

So as to change it – To rearrange
　　There is a proper order for everything
Be it happy sad or strange
　　Folk used to conversate together
Eye to eye and face to face
　　Then the great littleness of the machine came
Turned humanism into disgrace
　　And thus continues to this day

Maybe we need
　　To take the e-mail and the text
Study hard – Read between the lines
　　And really see what is coming next
All that is left is prayer and faith
　　And just a little bit of time
To make it right again …

Whatever happened to the person in me
    That lived for love and adventure
Musician – Poet and Teacher
    Pilgrim and sometime Preacher
With a penchant for being stoned
        (and Loving it)

Looking hard – Trying profoundly to see
    Why that went away – And when
Find the day and date – And contemplate
    Get the answers down – And then
Take myself on back home
    'Cause right now I am feeling
Useless – Olde – and Extremely Alone
    (and I really miss my friends)

Wake up in a cold sweat
    In the dead of the night
Nothing but yourself and the Truth
    Nowhere to run – No way to fight
Not a Goddamned thing that you can do
    Except try to fall back into sleep
        (and wonder)

What happened to that person
    Living for love and adventure
Really need to find out – Where has he gone
    Get back into myself – Before it is too late
Pray and contemplate – And carry on …

People will come into your life and
    Then abruptly they will go
On rare occasion they will stay awhile
    But you can never really know
Often it's a test of faith
    And all that you can do is
Put your heart on the chopping block
    And attempt to follow through …

There is a purpose to everything
    Another lesson to be learned
It is not always pretty – Can bring you down
    Especially when you get burned
By those you have taught yourself to care about …

When you love someone – You love them warts and all
    But you know that lies, deceit, and larceny
Always precede the fall
    Of things that could have mattered
But were just not meant to be
    Leave the spirit beaten down and tattered
Which is a temporary thing
    But out here – Temporary can be awhile …

With that aside – Here's to Love – And living it
    To being hurt – and Forgiving it
To finding the Truth – and to Treasure it
    To the beautiful dawn of a brand new day …
                    Never Give Up

I like to take the time to contemplate
    To sit about and wonder
As I watch the lightning in the sky
    And listen to the sound of the thunder ...

Thinking back on the good times
    About my family and true friends
How Love is spiritual and never dies
    Goes on Forever – Will never end ...

In those moments I can find
    The essence of my spirit and
Through the strength of the heart
    Have some peace of mind
There is a price we pay – Every day
    To keep from turning into cynics
All one can do is persevere – Until they find
    The lightning and the thunder
And the reason why ...

People play their silly games
    The children – They are caught right in between
Right and wrong – Good or bad
    Forced to choose – Is it Mom or Dad
For a child – Just hurts very deeply
    You know what I mean
Like putting the foot to a wounded animal
    Unforgivable – Makes you want to scream
As a Lion would roar at Winter …

Never too young that they do not remember
    And they carry these scars all of their lives
Why is it that no one ever contemplates this Truth
    Especially the husbands and wives
Who now are first and foremost – Mother and Father
    And still they argue and they threaten and they scream
Soon the innocent children are feeling that they are to blame
    And it messes up everything
Yet another child hurt – distrustful – and sad …

Suffer the little children
    Allow – Provide – And Love
This is Wisdom – A pure and simple Truth
    Given from the Lord above …
            Peace

Trapped — Between two realms of Existence
In the Middle
The primordial light of Infinity
And the black abyss of eternal Darkness
Where the Truth is self-realization
And it is the definition of Profound ...

Not a pretty thing by any means
Yet it has to be — For one to finally know
To see the brute simplicity of Cosmic things
Then to say goodbye — And let it go
To flow away on the river of Endless Times
You have to let it go ...

Two Native American princesses
    A visit from Friends
Souls I had imagined
    I'd not lay eyes on again
'Til we were all of us
    On the other side ...

For one it had been years
    The other, many more
It was like nobody had ever left
    Minutes after they came in
Through the door ...

We have all lived many lifetimes
    That sent us on our separate ways
And yet here we sit
    Many decades later
And realize the
    One thing that can never change
Is the Love one is blessed with through
    True Friendship
It is Eternal – It does not die ...

All of us had our doubt
    The Great Spirit brought our visit about
And there is but one lone solitary reason why
    We all of us needed it – Faith
To re-affirm
    The Love of kindred Spirits ...

        Life is just GRAND sometimes ...

The Children

Keep them close and keep it real
Make sure they always know
That they are Loved and Wanted and Special
That Love will never die or go
Stays with you through Infinity
Forever and a day
It is all we have – So teach them
They will listen to what you say
And they will remember …

Thanks, But No Thanks

I don't anymore
But back in the past
I did – And I did it right
Shots fired
Liquor and blood on the wall
Locked and loaded
Put some colour in the night and
Push On . . .

I got older – And tired of the bullshit
All the wanna-be's and man-pussies around
Women – I've been celibate for many years
Had my time with the finest
Then was wise enough to put it down
To just leave – And push on . . .

Folk today – In love with their misery
Ever'body got some jive-ass excuse
For not doing what they need to
Always at other's expense
These chumps can't even spell "Abuse"
And so
I just don't anymore . . .

G'Day

The Truth is there
　　Beating your Spirit about
The head and shoulders
　　Trying to make you
Open your eyes and see
　　But you pay it no heed
You are blinded by greed
　　In a prison
When you could be free ...

Your world exists in a computer screen
　　Won't look three inches
Past your nose – And we are steadily
　　Losing our Humanity
The book is about to close ...

Time to wake up
　　And smell the roses and
That is just the way it lays
　　Get it done while there is still some time
That is all there is to say ...

You figure you have some answers
    Been about it for quite awhile
But all that experience now seems as nothing
    You feel lost and alone – As a child
All you now seem aware of is
    That when you finally go
The end will be forevermore and
    No one ever really knows
Until they themselves pass through the door
        Of Infinity ...

For myself there is some fear in this honesty
    And I am searching for a power that
I pray will admonish me and
    Grant me the wisdom
To find my way home – Finally to have some peace
    And in the serenity to have the answers I need
To set my spirit free ...

Down here – Only a couple of minutes
    Out there is the second eternity
Awaiting us all – Do we rise or do we fall
    Are we blind or do we see
Will it be nothing – Or everything ...

These questions are now all that matter
    The answers I so much need to find
So that when it comes time for this short journey to end
    I can let it go – With peace of mind ...

Life ...
    All it is – All it ever was – All it will continue to be
Is just a small break you get – To smell the roses and such
    Between the two eternities ...

Sometimes I sit back – Try hard to see
   The real meaning of life and how it applies to me.

So many misgivings – About how it will end
   I am closing in on it – Is it a foe or a friend or
      Just the most natural of things …

You do the best you can do – With what you have got
Sometimes it works out – Other times it does not.

      Never give up – Always push on.
   Accept that it is a hit and miss thing, just like
       Composing a song, so
       Get on along with it …

Names – Like people
    Come and go away
But I never forget a face
    If you look into the eyes
The truth of the soul is there
    From that Infinite other place

Step back and take a look at yourself
    And tell me what you see
The Truth is there
    Hidden behind the Lie
And is waiting to set you free
    If you will allow it

Laughing or crying are the same release
    Joy nothing more than
The opposite side of grief
    Like taking happiness and
Turning it inside out
    It helps to teach one lessons
Which is what it's all about
    And time does not wait for anyone

The Truth is in the Eyes ...

Sometimes it just rips you
Cuts right to the heart,
Alone with nothing to do
But sit back and contemplate
The things you have done
And wonder how you made it through…

You learn from experience
The Good and the Bad
It all equals out in the end
And it is all going to pass
Except for your Soul
So you best get it done, while you can …

You do what you have to
In order to survive, and
You wind up where you are
Believe that the darkest hour comes before the Dawn
And the light of the Morning Star
And the Sunrise, to take you Home …

You cannot live your life by catering
    To other people and their whims
In the end it turns into nothing but
    A waste of time – That
You were meant to spend to
    Find the Truth – Through
Prayer and Contemplation
    To find your own unique Salvation
And some peace of mind …

Until you truly know thyself
    You cannot be genuine with anyone else
Turns into nothing more than a charade – A silly game
    At best – A transparent facsimile of the real thing
That always ends in nothing more than grief and pain …

So find yourself and make your peace
    Best do it while you can
This bit of time between eternities
    Is given to formulate a plan
And realize that when we pass
    We merge and become as one
To travel off into forever – Like rays travel from the Sun …

We are all getting older, and
Time does not wait.
Here to find the lesson and learn,
Before it is too late.

The answers are there for
Every one of us.
Open, like a book.
All that is needed is the courage,
To stop and take a look.

Stay true to thyself.
Know real love comes only once.
If it is lost, what comes after is mostly pretending.
The years go by and things wrinkle and fade, with
The exception being love, which is
Pure and Never-ending.
A Treasure.

And, there it is ....

So many people
"Lost" in their phone
No interaction with others
They just want to be alone with
The optical delusion of
The Machine.
Most completely unaware they are
Losing the essence, the very thing
That makes us human.
And nobody seems to care ...

Family out to dinner in a restaurant,
Good food but no "chat."
Each person with their "machine" in use,
Table is silent, like a big old cat.
Sneaking up behind its prey, to
Deliver the fatal blow.
Hear what I say — Heed the message,
There is still some time, you know,
To put it right again — And survive ...

I keep away from people
Mostly, they bring me down.

I keep company with
The animals and the birds.

With every other creature
I find comfort and simple truths.

With man – One thing comes to mind – One word.
"Abomination."

Up before daybreak
   To contemplate and pray
Seeking courage and a reason
   To endure another day ...

Been alone for awhile now
   Still have people all around
Yet for me it does not matter
   My spirit is breaking down
All of the colour is gone ...

Need to strengthen my faith
   That I might see beyond death
To know in my heart
   When I take my last breath
That dying is nothing
   That the soul carries on
That forever is infinite
   And those already gone
Are waiting for me
   To finally come home ...

The original Native American People
    Here living an excellent and prosperous life
Then the men with forked tongues
    And "Manifest Destiny" came
Killed off the food supply
    Brought smallpox, cholera, and strife
And did it in the name of God ...

So the Tribes gave up the land
    Moved northward and west
The hunting was good
    There was time to be thankful, to rest
And just when it seemed
    All things had worked out for the best
The white man found gold
    In the sacred Black Hills ...

Treaties sworn to in good faith
    Accepted by the tribes
Now were cast asunder on the "Yellow Rock"
    No place left to run or hide
So each chief summoned their warriors – Then took stock
    And the nations went to war
Many people began to die
    And there would be many, many more ...

The killing started in earnest at the Little Big Horn
    White soldier cowards finished it out at Wounded Knee
Women and children, old men and dogs
    Fuck "Manifest Destiny"
And do it in the name of God ...

Reflections

Like to see her one more time
Attempt to bring about
An understanding of what happened
So that we could see
Both of us were looking at the same thing
There is no doubt
She just saw it a bit differently than me…

As there are different shades of a colour
There are many variances in life as well
When one teaches – They also learn
To find faith and the inner strength to quell
The fear that abides in all of us
This is the meaning of true courage
To find the bravery to overcome
To fortify and nourish
The essence of the Soul…

As I sit to rest and contemplate
On occasion – I reflect
About the music – Full of promise – That we made
And for the life of me
I have yet to find a reason that it went so wrong
Same colour – 'Twas just a different shade…

Lines for the Times

Help me to find true faith, the
Faith that looks through Death ...

Laughing or crying is the same release
Joy is surviving the pain and grief
Of living ...

Flawless and gone, like a good blues song ...

Man does not live by bread alone, but
You can't make a sandwich without it ...

Names – Like people – Come and go away
But I never forget a face
If you really look into the eyes
The Truth of the Soul is there
From that Infinite other place ...

So step back and take a look at yourself, and
Tell me what you see
The Truth is there – Hidden behind the Lie
And is waiting to set you free
If you will allow it ...

It is exactly what it is
That is all it can ever be
M'self, I am long past wasting time so
I beg that you will pardon me but
I must take my leave…

There are many paths one follows to
Complete the journey here
High roads – Low roads – or No roads at all
Joy – Pain – and Fear
M'self, I hate to loiter
Keep on pushing it – Rise or fall
Trying to reconnoiter
What lies beyond the wall…

One carries on until it is over
Aware that for each of us the time must come
Illusion or delusion – All of it will finally end
Nowhere to hide – No place to run
Except to pass on through – Rise or Fall
Forevermore on the infinite side of
The Wall…

Which is exactly what it is and
All that it ever will be…

You know there are some things
    That money can't buy
Take care of each other and forget about why
    Life here is but an eye blink
In the infinence of time
    Love is the only thing that will survive
Eternally sublime

        This is Truth
        This is Wisdom
      Commit it to your Heart
     Keep your Faith and Push On
     Know you will never be apart
       Even when you are

Saddest people I have so far seen are
    Those that seem to have everything
Except for real Love and Trust – A compassionate Heart
    No retail or wholesale – No not any part
It is not a monetary thing
    Cannot put a price on it – You know exactly what I mean

      So take this Truth
       This Wisdom
     Commit it to your Heart
   Love is the only thing that will survive
     You will never be apart...

What is on the other side
    What is there to find
Is it everything – Or nothing
    Do we see – Or are we blind

It is said we will be known forever
    By the tracks we leave behind
One may not think this true
    But down the line – Time comes you find
That in point of fact – It does apply to you
    To each and every one of us
And all that we can do is
    Accept the Truth – And get on with our lives

To try our best not to fall prey
    To all those stereotypical roles
Nothing down here really means anything
    Except for Love and Faith and Soul

I know the one line I do not want to sing
    When it comes my time to go – Is
"Nothing but dark – Can't see a goddamned thing"
    Work on keeping the faith – Don't you know

All we ever really have
    Is Love and Faith and Soul …

Here's to the Fathers
Deserving of the name
Who did the best they could
With what they had
Willing to give up everything
If called upon
Except for the Love of the children
That know him as "Dad..."

Happy Father's Day

I will not Forget ...

When you have lived many years
    There comes a time
Where it seems as though
    Death is like a season
Every other day someone has died
    "May their soul have been in heaven
Three hours 'fore the devil knew them dead"
    You scream – And then later
You take a private moment – And you cry …

Know that many have gone before
    And many will come after
Each and every one of us
    Must take our due
And that can be a fearful thing
    To think about at times
When in your heart you know
    Time is closing in on you …

Try to find some answers
    Ponder what I might say
When my turn comes – To look death in the eye
    Will she appear as a beautiful angel
Or my worst nightmare – Gone awry
    And will I have the faith
To get me through it – Either way …

When I close in on time – and time "closes" me …

The very souls that I love so deeply
   Have been the one's I have hurt the most
Defies all logic and explanation
   At least that I can see
Feel like I have murdered, cheated,
   Stolen, lied, and walked off from my brethren
When way down deep inside
   I know that isn't me ...

Knock and you may enter
   Seek and you will find
Emotions ripped and shattered along the way
   My faith yet still sustains me
That faith is all that now remains
   It has been a long time
Since I stopped caring about why
   Just pushing on — Awaiting my time to die ...

And join my friends
Waiting for me
At the Rainbow Bridge ...

On Violence

Violence attends growth and
 The right or wrong of it is dependent
  On individual perception. Is it (violence) a
   Necessary agent of change or a needless
    Usurpation of Law?

On "The Third of the 'Herd' Guys"

They were all "way up boys."
 Gentlemen of the "first water."
  No better will be found.
And that goes as it lays, by God ...

Don't know why the Spirit moves me
    The way it sometimes do
Don't have a clue — But I listen to my heart
    For me - Reality is the other side of
This delusion known as life — We all get to die
    And for every ending — There will be another start ...

People say I'm crazy — That I rave on like a fool
    My Faith — It's getting tested all the time
Folk care more about their phones
    Than they do about each other
Talking about all these "virtual" visions but
    To Life's truths — They are blind
Enough to make a soul just want to break down and cry ...

So I keep a lot to myself — Alone with the music
    On occasion I'll be writing things down
Gave up on the superficial many years ago
    The olde "Corporate Fuck Around"
Working good people on empty promises
    Bosses lining their pockets with gold
The rich keep getting richer — Care only for themselves
    The rest of us — We just keep getting old ...

Say I don't know why my Spirit
    Sometimes do me like it do
But I plan to keep on listening to my heart
    Going to keep on a'seeking — Until I find
For every ending — There will be
    A Brand New Start ...

It is coming – Closing in and
    And I can feel it
There are magnitudes of thoughts
    Running wildly through my head
But the one thing I can't put my finger on
    Nor see off in the distance is
Any notion whatsoever – No sign of any dread
    Of the way it has to be …

I wonder if – When my time finally comes
    Will I look death in the eye
Say a prayer – And blow a kiss and
    With a smile – Lay down and die
Giving thanks to the Great Power
    For the many lives I got to live
Then just let it be and start my journey
    To find the Rainbow Bridge
And be with those who love me – Once again …

The truth is there
    Beating your spirit about the head and shoulders
Trying to make you open your eyes and see
    But you pay it no heed
You are blinded by greed
    In a prison – When you could be free ...

Your world exists in a computer screen
    Will not look three inches past your nose
And we are steadily losing what is left of our humanity
    The great book of life is about to close
Time to wake up and smell the roses

    And that is just the way it lays ...

Every one of us
   Has at one time or another known
      Someone in love with their own pain
Get so wrapped up in their own imagined misery
      Start to treating others with disdain.

There is an art and a beauty to all that exists
   Some folk will not allow themselves to see
      The truth is so fundamentally simple
      The word is synchronicity.

With all that surrounds us
   In everything that we do
      There are consequences, good and bad
Sometime or another we all get to sing the blues
      But joy is just the other side of sad.

We all get to feel it
   In point of fact we need it
      Without the one you cannot appreciate the other
Time to stop feeling sorry for ourselves
      And interact once more with our sisters and brothers

Learn the meaning of love again
   Not selfish, but giving
Having the faith when the time comes to
   Let go of this thing we call living
And be able to do it with a smile…

Oil and toxic chemicals
    In the water that we drink
Genetic manipulation of the food we eat
    Whole species of plants and animals
Extinct – Due to the pollution
    That was introduced as a solution
It should make us think ...

That it might be conducive
    For us to find another way
There's not a lot of time left
    "Only so many hours in a day"
All things must pass
    And they most certainly will
This madness has to end
    While we have the time still ...

To do something about it
    Maybe even to save
Get rid of the poison – And the lies
    Lay the foundation
For a Brand New Day
    While there is time
While there is time ...

So hard to be alone
    It drives me wild
I feel so lost
    Just like a little child
My best friend left me
    He had to go
A lot of me died with him
    And I just don't know
Not anymore – Not anymore …

I had to be strong for him
    He gave me a reason
We went through so much
    Then like the passing of a season
He was gone …

Free now – In another place
    Where there is no pain, hardship, or strife
Forever young again and everlasting
    In the state of Eternal Life …

    Peace, my little friend …

I am a bit worried, Great Father
    Grant me the strength and wisdom
        To stay the course
           Please ...

I can sense it coming
    Just around the bend
And I am trying hard at acceptance
    To realize in my heart and soul
That all things here will end and
    Hope that if I have a preference – That
The journey through the
    Second of the two eternities
Will begin at the Rainbow Bridge ...

Say the day is going to come
    There won't be a need anymore
Humanity is gone
    In a jar on some lab shelf
Behind closed doors

And we did it to ourselves
    By allowing it to be
The fault belongs to nothing else
    But you and them and me

Man is supposed to use the machine
    Now it is the machine
That is using man
    Taking a little bit more each and every time
You are holding the "Smart Phone" in hand
    What we do not use – We are losing
Refuse to see the writing on the wall
    If we let it take us down
There is no "Re-boot" – No coming back
    Of course
That has been "Big Brother's" plan all along …,

Sometimes I get scared and
It is not fleeting
Hangs with me like a bad cold
Like taking a severe beating,
From something that is not even there
Seems no one really gives a shit
Which is saying that nobody cares ...

Ever'body got some kind of fear
The thing is being brave
Having the guts to find the
Courage to push on
This is what separates the wheat from the chaff
The sole difference between weak and strong ...

All you can do is
Be true to yourself
Come to terms with that thing deep inside
Walk through the door and
Just let it be
Let your soul once again be your guide, and
Take you back where you belong ...

To lose something or
Someone that you feel defines you
When it seems all that is left is
The history now behind you
Accept that for a bit of time
The pain of your grief will blind you . . .

Look to your faith
To the infinite truth of love
Know that all other things will pass . . .

Be Blessed and Push On.

To Melanie. God Bless. We will not forget.
See you soon . . .

Sit about and watch things
  Am bothered by what I see
This class that are called people now
  Are not really human beings ...

Forgotten how to love
  Most cannot even spell compassion
Live life engulfed in a computer screen
  'Cause that's the latest fashion ...

    Such a pity.

For the "Plebes"

There are many little intricate and delicate things –
Bring the mightiest of warriors down on their knees.

Always stay ahead of yourself –
And look for the lesson.

This is Wisdom.

It is said that laughing or crying are
The same release
Joy is surviving the pain and the grief of
Living and trying to
Keep the love intact
Once it is smashed into pieces
You do not get it back ...

So

I do my best to persevere and to
Learn the things I must
So that when this all ends
I will find my friends in that other place
And trust
In God and my Faith
They will be there ...

Aware of the absurdity
         A lot more than I used to be
All one has to do is step outside
         It hits you in the face
The spirit recoils in disgrace
         What a waste – and for m'self
Found only one place I can hide

Which is why these days
         I spend a lot of time alone
Works out so much better anyway
         Can't see people's faces for
Their goddamned phones

 And there it is

Sitting alone – With thoughts that border with insanity
Roiling through the mind – No quarter
One must remember and most of all accept that
We are here to learn
The good – the bad – the ugly – All happen for a reason
For everything there is a season
And the circle forever turns – Unbroken

The sheer truth – The message of the ages
Is all around you – You have only to
Open the envelope – And begin to read the pages
To find the answers – To have some peace
In the midst of the insanity – The circle forever turns
Unbroken

There is an inherent beauty to everything
An infinite galaxy of the spiritual around it
You can look for it too hard and never see
When you just accept it on faith is when
You have found it

Faith is believing in something
You cannot touch or see
It is a "knowing" that you have inside
Like feeling joy or misery
Which are different sides of the very same coin
Continue on – And let it be
Inherently

Love your brother and take care of each other as
You journey toward the sun
Remember only love and the spirit are everlasting
All things merge and become as one
Then you can take it on home
Inherently

A split – Between all cultures
Overhead – The vultures
Circling 'round
Waiting for their turn
The orchestra plays
"The End of Days"
As the city of Babylon burns

Nobody cares – Nobody dares
Too many "robotic eyes" around
Video surveillance everywhere
Speak out – And they can track you down
Get too close to the truth
Then you might disappear
Operative word and tactic these days is
Nothing else but "Fear"

The city is now burning and
We brought it on ourselves
The Tower of Babel falls again – A victim of itself

What the "Geeks" do not see

Oh, "computer-speak" is now the language
Tells you what to say AND how to spell
Do not exercise the mind – It will be gone in short time
Which is why the whole damned world is
Going straight to hell

For each new "gigabyte" your mind uses to
Let "the machine" teach you another "short cut" trick
You lose "megabytes" of your spirit -- Do not get it back
It is enough to make one sick

Cannot see the trees for the woods

The rain, it falls
      Even as the sun doth shine
See their faces, in the mist
      The irony of things can confuse the mind
But it is alright, you insist
      As you walk along and wonder
'Bout things you should or might have done, but
      Long ago is a way back down the road
Not too much time remains here, my son

And when it is over, it is truly gone
      All you can do is try your best
To keep pushing on, and
      Be honest with yourself
Practice with others as well
      Do your best to make it right, then say
"Good night"

This particular reality is a dilemma
I am finding hard to any longer understand, to
The point I do not feel the need much anymore to have to
Tolerate the total insignificance of it all, to
Watch as a mere machine brings about
The demise of man
To the total ignorance of everyone, or
So it would seem

I make this observation
Not out of fear but consternation for
What has caused this "letting go" of
The things that really matter
World is cold enough as it is, without
Getting "gone against" by your own

Where did our humanity go?

I do not believe that I have the right to
Pass judgment on a man
Do not need another passing judgment on me
We all do the best that we can
All of us have things we don't want people to see
Some folk are not going to understand
Does not necessarily make it wrong
Sometimes things just do not go as planned

You have to do what you do
To pull yourself through and
And when "breathing" or not comes into question
You have to just let it go
Drop it fast
"Better him than us" is the pertinent suggestion

Sometimes things just do not go as planned.

Soul was just not right for the modernity of the day
Too many sacred customs a long time gone
"Traditional man" just another virtual scam
Perpetrated by a machine we now all depend on

Humanity cannot be replicated by the "machine"
Whose one basic purpose is to take away
The very essence of what makes people who they are or at least
Who and what they were "back in the day"

Sometimes it takes a catastrophe to
Stop one in their tracks and to finally see
The simple truth of it all
That modernity and technology past a certain degree
Are terminal

What is a person, without the soul?

'Bout Life

It is not all about "you" and "yourself," it's about
What gets sent through you in order
To help and nurture someone else

We all have separate paths that
We are sent here to follow, with
Intersects of other folk who are doing the same
When these trails come together, take time to pause and talk
To learn – To be blessed and – To gain

For a few moments at least
The serenity and peace, of
Sharing with your sisters and brothers
The Infinite Power of Love

I needed to drop the war
Find a whore, and
Top it off with a bump of "china white"
Inhale the smoke of mystic herb, and
Be alone with my spirit through the night

What I remember the most is me
Standing all alone on the coast
Absorbing the sun and the breeze from the sea
A mere teenager in Southeast Asia
On the shore thanking God, for
Allowing it to be

Vietnam Republic, circa 1969
(boy, was I in for some "surprises")

Death
    It is always in front of us
Waiting
        Choices made years ago
        Out of ignorance or otherwise
        Rear their ugly heads years later
To smile
        To remind us of the coming darkness

Is it all for naught or is
        This small span of time we have bought just
         A classroom for mistakes
        To teach
        To learn
        To discern

Does it even make a difference
        What comes after

Death
Waiting
        The final, ultimate frontier

When I get lonely – What I try to do is
Think about good things – 'Bout me and you
All the things we felt together – All the best times that we had
Then I remember that you left – Makes my heart sad

(chorus)

Try to figure what happened – Try to find a way
Bring us back together – Where we need to be
And stay

Now that I'm older – Settled down
See that life is just another circle – Constantly spinning 'round
Without the pain I could not feel – The depth of the joys we had
Now I know that it was real – Makes my heart sad

(repeat chorus)

Yet I have the memories – And with their strength my spirit carries on
I believe somehow someplace – We stand together – Still
I close my eyes – I see your face and it soothes my soul
What we had is out there – Never ending
Like to "bring it on back home"
Want so bad to bring it on back home

(fade & fini)

Sometimes people mistake me – Think I am something I'm not
When the realization comes that they were wrong – They hate me
So these days me, myself, and I is what I've got, and
The three of us keep moving – On down the road

A man's word – Don't mean a thing – Not anymore
Cannot look a person in the eyes and talk
Can't see their faces for the phone
Off in some "virtual world" alone
That's when the three of us – Me, myself, and I – Go for a walk

Politicians rattle on – Making promises they never keep
New "Technology" running mankind into the ground
Take away our spirit – The right to work it out ourselves
Will not like the result if we allow it to come around
Be "Too wet to plow" – The wall going to come tumbling down

That is why me, myself, and I – Just the three of us keep moving
On down the road

I do not fall sway to "Love" anymore
Except for animals – The gifts of nature – And my daughter
Eight years now in abstinence
Got my fill of going through the emotional slaughter
That comes with that particular four letter word

Oh, we can talk – We can drink – Share some smoke – Sit back and think
Discuss the relative issues of the day
Do anything up to [and ending at] – "I love you so much"
On that subject – There is not much more to say
Been there – Done that – A number of times
Finally wore out – Got tired of playing games
Keep moving on

Once, maybe twice – Oh, we were there
In "Love's Eternal Bliss"
The rest of it was nothing more than pretending
Sometimes even that was good – But one thing never changes
Each beginning has an ending – It has been that way through the ages
Which keep moving on

All I am saying – In the present vernacular
Is simply – If it is not going to be at the least – Spectacular
Believe I'm going to have to pass – And keep moving on down the line

Adieu

Short & Sweet

Wake up startled in
The middle of the night
Try to put it all together
So I sit and write
Put thoughts down to paper
Try hard to see
Some reason for this madness
That exists in me
So far – To no avail.

I have only one question
Can you answer it my friend
Exactly who was inside of that uniform and
Why did his life have to end

Big countries use small countries
To propagate the spread of
Logistical nightmares of war that
Bring them wealth and
Leave many thousands dead
While the rest of us keep getting old

Take our children – Still fresh and young
Fill their minds with dreams
Teach what an honor it is to die for some bogus ideal
Then put them in a pretty uniform – On to the battlefield
To feel the bullet sting them
To wonder if any of it was real – As they die
Do they wonder "why"

Again – I have only one question
Can you answer it my friend
Exactly who was inside of that uniform
And why did his life have to end

Would for us to go away and
Sail upon the oceans
Never to look back nor say a word
'Bout what is left behind of
Useless preconceived notions
'Cause it's not there for us – Not anymore

We are on our way to find
The truth of ourselves again – The "realness" of being
Where instead of just looking
One is actually "seeing"
The way that it really is
Has always been
And is always going to be
The three of us together
God, and you, and me
Finally

I'm doing everything
That I can do
Trying hard to get
Back home to you

Know now the only place
That things went wrong
Was with me

Now I awaken in the middle of the night
Cannot understand how I lost sight
Of the beauty that was there
Shining like the sun – So very bright
Around you

Want so badly to come home
Tired of doing it alone
I see your face in everything I try to do
Want so very much to find a way
To bring it all back where it belongs
Not too much more I need to say
I carry on

The Government – It rapes you – They "siliconvalleyate" you
Take a little more of your soul every day
Plan being to "thin us out" a bit – While they fill our heads with shit
Take our money – Quell our rights – Then you hear them say
"Everything is fine – Don't want to lose your place in line"
Big Brother – Oh, he's going to "take good care of you"
While "The Machine" corrupts your brain – Then they put you on "the train"
And that's the end of it – Over, done – You're through – Long gone

"Common Folk" walk around today – "Smart Phone" three inches from their noses
As if blind – They don't see a goddamned thing
Killer viruses and plagues – Top Secret meetings at The Hague
Far from some "virtual" bed of roses – On a computer screen

Premiers and Presidents – Prime Ministers and their Cabinets
All gather about – Join hands and sing
Of how they took "the masses" down – With so very little effort
Then they all bow – To praise and worship – "The Machine"

Technology gone terminal – Destroyed us again
And the blame is no one else's but our own
'Course no one's going to listen – Don't have the foresight or the time
All too busy – Fornicating with their phones

Adieu

Let us all bow down with humility
Offer up our virtual prayers to the sky
To the "Great Computer Whore" whose sole utility
Is ensuring that "humanity" dies – Spiritless – Wasted – and Abused
Do no good – (Even if we could) – To wonder why
The "Omnipotent Machine" does not allow it

Sadly enough – We brought it on ourselves
Lost our Spirituality – And the "Grit"
To rise up in anger – To raise the sword
To overcome and destroy – Such petty shit
That has now been allowed to turn into a monster
To decimate and devour our very souls

It was said back in the day – When man was still "aware" of such things
That pure evil would come disguised as an angel of light
To "woo and cajole" one into the blasphemous abomination
That God does not exist – There is no wrong or no right
Now – There is only "The Machine"
And that minuscule "chip" in your wrist – The "Mark of the Beast"
"E-read" the Book of Revelations
You will see exactly what I mean

Adieu

"Allo?"

Is anyone here old enough
To remember when a promise meant something
Like a warm fire on a cold December day
Or to sit together and talk – To just "be" with each other
Attempt to figure out a way
To make things better?

Back when you could look a person in the eye
Feel the power in their word
Know that they would rather die – Than to break it
And on the rare occasion that one was unable to "carry through"
They would "look you up" and let you know
Giving you ample time to take it and
Turn it 'round in spite of – Make it all come out alright

Used to be – Back in the past
The way "good folk" would do
When did that integral part of being human disappear
That is the question needing answered
So I am asking you – Is anyone here old enough to remember
When it all meant something?

Eh?

I refuse to apologize
For what I am,
For my strengths or absurdities,
If I had it to do again
I would not change a thing,
Because all of that, "The Journey"
Is in and of itself
Quite specifically the reason I am "me."

Know that I offend at times
Those that I care for most,
Can only hope they realize there's no personal intent
Sometime though, I have to "blow it out"
Get "shed of it" and vent,
Even when those I love the best are close.

Finally see the reason for the way things are,
Forget about personal gain,
Know that simplicity is fundamental for Peace of Mind, and
Technology, past a certain point, the sum root of grief and pain.
As it has always been, and will be forevermore, and
Man's mistake, our great sin, is
Closing our eyes to the truth of things, by feigning blindness.

Again, for those I love the most, there is no personal intent,
Sometime though, when overwhelmed I have to "blow it out" and vent. Be Blessed.

I just roll with it as it comes and goes
Anymore, hell, don't even know if I care to substantiate,
Had a memorable run and a lot of fun,
Known both ends (in the extreme) of love and hate.
Yet even with the bad times, most of it has been good to great, and
Without some hurt and pain,
How are you going to ever really know?

Got tangled up awhile back "Living the Lie,"
Making promises I never intended to keep,
Hurt the people I loved best the most, then
They died and left my soul to weep.
Before I could set things right,
Still haunts my spirit in the dead of the night.
Makes me wonder and pray
Not to allow such as that to ever happen anymore,
With those treasured few that remain.

And yet, without the grief, how are you ever going to know the joy
That is the other side of the very same coin?
Roll with it as it goes, all that you can really do, is to take it as it comes.
Fundamental Simplicity.
Eternity

We have allowed "Technology"
To break us down, and
To steal our humanity.
Love and Compassion – Are no longer in fashion,
Life is now dictated and run by "The Machine."

The "Great Computer" rules
Over a world of fools, all
Running about with their
Eyes glued to a "screen,"
Exuding nothing more than a virtual lie, and
Leaving the Truth, sight unseen.

Which has been the "plan" all along.
"Mechanized Deception," brought to perfection,
The fundamental reality of Life,
Destroyed and gone.

And we did it to ourselves.

So Anyway;

Birds out feeding on the patio,
Shaman dog is on his mat,
Drum kit all over the living room,
I am exactly where I need to be at.

Write the words that come to me,
From where, I do not know,
A lot of times they turn into songs,
The Blues, and Rock and Roll.

Most often sunrise comes as my reminder,
It is time for me to rest,
I pray, meditate, and grab some sleep,
Then get up and do my best
To "Push On" in a positive way, although at times I must confess,
It's a tough row to hoe, I'm saying
Life here can really be a mess, and that's why
The birds, the dog, the music,
They never lie to me, or let me down,
I rate them right up there with praying,
Love is a circle, spinning 'round, and never ending.
The Truth will never let one down.

Henri and Tennis T

White Lincoln Continental,
Poached eggs with Turkish hash,
So drunk in the sand on the coastline,
We missed the whole damned tennis match.

"Betty White" was our lady,
Doing both of us all the time,
Neither of us cared at all though,
'Cause she was eighty percent "Fine."

Discos, bars, "Umberto's Clam House,"
Stretch limo in New York City,
"Little Italy" and the Terelli sisters,
We were sure 'nuff "Livin' Pretty," and
Thought it would never end, yet it had to.

But here we sit, decades down the road,
Got our separate lives, but still fast friends,
Still laughing and talking about memories
No one can ever tarnish or take away.

"Thought it would never end," and it didn't ever really.
To a "Brother," Peace.

There is the "Economy of Nature,"
Of which we are a part, and
The "economy of man" which is
"Expansion" and "Capital Gain,"
At any and all costs, no matter what is lost,
How is it that "Progress" should
Cause such suffering and pain?
How much longer can the
Earth and the environment sustain,
With all the poison, pollution, and greed
Put upon her for "power" and "money,"
Which are no more than optical delusions none of us need.

Each of Nature's Creations,
From the great lion to the tiny ant,
Are here for a specific reason, as are
The trees and other plants, and
There is a delicate harmonic balance
That if man does not soon pay attention to,
Will fall away and bring the "End of Days," and
There will be nothing left to do,
But gnash our teeth and wish we had, when we still had time,
Adieu.

At least three different viruses
Loosed like a plague,
The "insides" drop right out of your ass.
"Oh, we have a 'vaccine' that will keep you alive,"
Believe I'm going to have to pass.
Know what I mean?
Hear what I'm saying?
This is one serious little game we are playing.

Are we ever going to learn?
Am beginning to doubt it. Looks like
Nobody really gives a damn about it, as we
Approach the End of Days.

Dog assed tired, yet
I still won't sleep,
Memories haunt me, but
I do not weep.
I make war,
Do battle on my drums, so
I do not have to take it elsewhere and
Nobody has to run.
It works for me.

Soft spring breeze, it whispers the names of
Loved ones, a long time gone.
In my recollections now, forgotten a lot of the pain,
I feel them smiling, and know they are pushing on,
Out there, somewhere.

Then comes the time of the Irony, the devastation of it all, and
It comes with a vengeance, breaking like a wave,
As a never ending fall.

So I make war and do battle on my drums, so that
I do not have to take it elsewhere, and
Nobody has to run. It works for me.

Fini.

The young lady could sing, and
I mean do it really good, and
Looked like she was created in "Hollywood."
Everything in the world that a person would need, to
Hit the "Big Time" and have all the dailies read,
"A Star is Born."

Why she let it go I will never know,
'Cause she could sing like a bird, sent from heaven.

We had gotten so close, and from so far away, and
It was in fact, the power of Spirit, and
There is really nothing more to say, except
What happened to the magic,
Did we get in too close, too near it?

It was right there in her hands, and I cannot understand, 'cause
She could sing like a beautiful bird,
Come down from Heaven.

On my own and still running,
Back to the drums, instead of "hired gunning."
Keeps me happy, what can I say?
Love the Blues and Rock and Roll,
I do it every day.

Way back in the distance,
I did the soldiering thing,
At the time, "covert" paid a lot of money.
Afterwards, I drove the "Big Trucks" over a million miles,
Had a hell of a good time doing that too, honey.

But music has always been my first love,
Getting back to m'drums and writing songs.
They say it comes full circle, and by God here it is, and
I continue to "carry it on."
Still upright, well, and raising hell, through
The power of the song.
My "fire" is in the music:
Keeps me going strong.

Heaven and Hell
Are right here on earth,
No need to die,
Both are available at birth.

Primordial light,
The black abyss of night,
Wrong and right,
And forever.

The purpose of life is to master these subjects
In a serious and infinite way,
Forever lasts quite a bit longer than
Every single night and day
That will ever come, or has ever been,
The day we start life is the dawn of sin.
Goes back to the "tree and the apple."

The End.

I wish
  I hope
    I pray
That we – All of us
  Will be together again some day
And please forgive me Great Father
  But I have to say, that
I hope it happens soon …

Faith is knowing but
  Being unable to touch or see
As when a soft wind blows and
  I know you are speaking to me
The warmth of the sun upon my face
  Is like the spiritual energy – Shining always
Radiant from another place
  Across the Rainbow Bridge …

    I wish
      I hope
        I pray

And await the final leap
  Of Faith …

You have your own little world
    That you try hard to stay in
Away from the turmoil and strife
    All the lies and the cheaters
The child and wife beaters
    Alone is better than living that life …

Walked about in those places
    Back in the day
Certain you had the strength
    To overcome it
That with the power of love
    You could beat it all down
But the truth turned out to be
    Far from it …

So that reality you were living
    You just had to leave
Here now you play music and write
    No one is saying that it is not hard
It is tough being alone with yourself some nights
    But for me it is so much better
Than living that life …

    Such an "Optical Delusion."

The
SLAM IT DOWN BLUES
Song

Say it ain't nothing but a thing – And
It really shouldn't matter
Just adds a little more stink to the
Bullshit already on the platter
That I really didn't need

Gets to the point sometime in life – Where
You feel you have seen it all before – And
Then out of nowhere – You are swept
Off of your feet – As a sheer vision
Appears in the door

To Tempt – To Tease – To Hurt – To Please
So naïve in her youth – Yet
So very charming to behold
Blonde – Blue Eyed – and Magnificent
As a Goddess from Days of Olde

But as time goes by – You begin to see
That maybe things are not
Quite what they seem to be
Petty manipulation breaks down
To just a "con" – And
It hurts when a lie is what
You based everything on – So
You pick up the few parts of
Your heart that are left – That
Were not the victims of
This woman's latest theft – And
Wonder out your lifetime
In a shelter made of stone
Surrounds the heart – No misery
The truth need not be known

I saw the signs and ignored them all
So it is nobody's fault
But my own

10 July, 2008

You and I came upon each other at a time
In our lives when no one else wanted
Either of the two of us.

Yes my little friend, Fate put us together,
And by God, we stuck like glue.
"Perma-Bond," you hear?

We will always be together, Dakota.
We share the same Soul, you and I.
I will see you again.
I know what I saw.
Love you buddy,
See you soon.

08 October, 2014

As did you and I. "The Shamus" and Thomas.
The same little "Tibetan Monk," same Spirit.
Just came back in a different "outfit."
A year today – I feel the same way.

Dakota – Shamus – Thomas
One total Soul.

I love you. See you soon.

The three of us, at the
RAINBOW BRIDGE.

PEACE

A Dog is just GOD coming at you backwards. Be Blessed.

84

There are scales and arpeggios, fundamentals and
Rudiments and different techniques.
And there is the actual guttural, emotional aspect
Of playing in the context of the song or the band,
In the "Moment."

Two completely different animals.

My preference is "Live and Sporting."
That's where my "chops" really come together.

Out of that "seat of my pants" spontaneity is when
I start latching onto any licks, patterns, styles that
Are needed to make those "moments" spectacular.

For me, "Live" is the Truth.
Comes straight from my Spirit.
It is what I do.
And Love.

"McScrotom" – 2008

"BLOOZE"

I'm sayin' show me some mercy there Percy
Play us some "Blooze" tonight
Then I'll go out and win the big lotto prize
And ever'thang will sho' nuff beeze alright

Big breasted lady on the dance floor
Say she be lookin' real hard at me
Got that "need" in her eyes
Sho' can wiggle those thighs — And
I know that she wants me to see
That it's "Game Time," boys and girls

Get crazy on the dance floor — Then
We slide on out to the car
Do some really wild things — That we couldn't
If we had stayed inside the bar
(That's all I'm sayin')
Then we go back inside — Throw down some "shooters"
Back out and feelin' no pain on the dance floor
Butt shakin' — Sweat all over those bodacious "hooters"
Sweet Jesus — Just can't ask fo' no more
(But I will)

Talkin' 'bout "Blooze" you can use Baby
Take you right on through the night
Still be all Bright-Eyed & Bushy-Tailed — Ready to Go
Come the Morning Light
Anyone for breakfast? — I know Dat's Right

So complicated,
   So hard to carry on.
Seems life gets
   Harder when you are weak,
And easy when you are strong.

It will catch you
   With your pants down, for
Those few seconds
   You are not looking, then
Friends and lovers and money go,
   Ain't got any food for cooking.
But the band keeps playing on.
   All of the answers , are
Right there, in the song.

It's just that
   Nobody seems to be listening.
The blood on the saber
   Still glistening.
Where did the time go,
   When people cared?
When life at least seemed fair?

Make you wonder,
   If it was ever really true, at all.

Sitting here and wondering
What it is I need to do
To make you aware of how it is
That the choice is up to you

You can try to understand it
And move on past the strife
You don't just reprimand the bandit
When they try to steal your life

You take them down

Love and hate are just different sides
Of the same coin that we all carry
Old men out riding Harley Super Glides
While their women lay in wait to parry
With the "tennis pro" or the "golfer guy"
To get "instruction" on how to swing
And I ain't just talkin' 'bout racquets and clubs
They're getting' that other "thing"

And the band plays on

Want you to know
That if you need to
You can always fall back on me
Yeah — There were some hard times
But lookin' back — That part of it is
Damned near impossible to see

What sticks in my mind and heart
Is all the joy and the good times we had
Be nice to revisit for a minute or two
A drink and some laughs
Would that be so bad

Anyway, said what I wanted to say
Here's to good and better days

A Friend

(This one done in "Tribute" to Gino, and his "Tony Bennet wanna be" persona.)
{the "depth" of a potato chip}

Such a pity – Such a shame
Some folk just don't get it
For them it's just a game of
"My way or the highway"
One more obsessive-compulsive scam
That shows you their "true colors"
That they don't really give a damn
'Bout anything but themselves

Legends in their own minds
Always taking – Never giving
Nothing but a bad joke
And still they think that
They are living
And it ain't nothing but a lie
There is no valid reason why
Except that it is what it is

Some do – Some don't
Some will – Some won't

Let go of the rot and
Push On

Find the Truth – It is out there

Time comes,
     A man has to find himself.
        He knows that he must leave home.
    Leave his family and friends behind,
      And tackle life alone.

    The only way to come around,
       To finally really see,
  Is just to let it all go and
       Find the strength you need
Within the depths of your soul.
      Before you run out of time.

    Life is just a break one gets
      Between the eternities.
  It is tough enough to find the truth.
      Don't need people 'round that lie to me.

    The answer is in the music.
      True friendship is a song.
To stand alone by the water and know this
      Is what helps me to carry on.

      Find Peace,
   While you still have some time.

Do what you do
Live and let live
Try hard not to take
Endeavor to give
Because it all comes back around

Some folk cannot see the trees
Because of the woods
And most times
It is a choice that they have made
But the bullets still fly
And people die
Most forgotten 'fore they're done
Fillin' in the grave

Cannot let it get back
To how it all used to be
Going to sleep under a bridge
Is just not for me
Never going down that road anymore
Got nothin' to do
With rich or poor
Just getting really tired of
All the bullshit floatin' around

Allo?

Intense is what I am
It lives in the drums when I play
It is present in everything that I do
It is how I find my way

Sometimes it is intense pleasure
Often it is intense pain
Either way – I'll take the full measure
You got to lose – So you can gain
And that is just the way it is

I don't need or have the urge
To be like anybody else
All I really want to do is
Stay true unto myself

Intensely so
'Tis the only way that I know
To push it on down the road

Do not need or have the urge
To be like anybody else
All I really care about is to
Stay true to myself

And in doing so – I find the Truth
And it helps me to get along
With my brethren and the creatures
Of the "World"
The Truth brings everything together
Like different musical notes
Turn into beautiful songs

Always comes up behind you,
The proverbial "thief in the night."
Not a damned thing you can do
About it at all,
Except to try to "put things right,"
Before it comes time to go.
Sooner or later, we all have to die.
I am going for the latter, but
One never knows.
HooAhh!

Different people,
> Different places,
Could be the way
> It was intended to be.
An example: Ebola has been around
> Since the nineteen seventies ,
Now it "visits" here
> To kill you and me.

{did I hear some idiot talking "Technology?"}

Make the 1918 flu pandemic,
> Cholera, even the "Plague,"
Look like a Sunday school picnic
> On a warm afternoon, and
The whole "deal" was
> "Planned and put in motion" at
The Hague.
> That's right.

It is not about racism, but
> It is about "Tribal."
Different countries, separate nations.
> No need to be rivals.
Just take care of your people, and
> Do it all from where you belong.
I will do the very same, and
> It will not be long,
It will get back to being as it was
> Intended to be.
Hear what I am saying?
> I am talking to thee.
It is all about "Tribes."

All I know is that I care
I also know that life isn't fair
At times you have no idea
About what to do
Except just rock-on and party and
Play some Blues

The love of my life
Is still yet a child
With only a slight idea of how it is
The angst of her youth
At times just drives me wild
In my quest to see the truth

Sometime we look so hard
That we cannot see
The way things really are
Until we take leave and travel
Look back in hindsight
From afar

And when it is all about to unravel
Is when the lesson is finally given
There are times you can fix things
And times that you can't
'Tis all just a part of living

And the beat goes on

The McArver Family

I think back to the times when we were all still here
And every one of us knew,
That no matter how bad or tough it might be,
Your family would be there for you.
And they never let me down. Ever.

Bought my first set of drums and Volkswagen car,
And allowed me to follow my dreams.
Bail me out of the jams I'd get myself in, sometimes
Requiring a big chunk of "green," as in money.

Piss my father off so bad, and break my mother's heart, but
We always found a way to work things out, and
In my journey I have used everything they taught me, and
Never doubted for a moment or had to worry about
The fact that they loved me.

My kid brother and I were close,
Although we had our fights, but
I saved his life and he sure enough saved mine, and
Together we spent many a night
With a bottle, a "doob," and each other — As brothers, and
By God, we did it right.

So here's to my family with all of my love,
Who even now gone are still with me for all time.
For my mother and dad, and for Michael,
The pleasure was all mine.

Peace, guys . . . Love

People come, and then they go
Sometime they stay – You never know
Take it as it comes – Push on and try
To find the answers – Before you die
And that is all that one can do

Access, profess, confess to a "screen,"
Pay homage to and worship
A goddamned "Machine."

"Computer-Speak" and "Spell-Check"
Change up the very words that you say,
The sole purpose being to
Wash the Truth of this life away, and
Disguise it all in a "virtual bed of roses."
{ Ah, "Technology."}

Plague{s} heretofore unknown to man
Thin out the population
An integral part of "The Plan,"
In the last fifteen years or so
Everyone with a "smart phone" in hand
Little mini computers, do you understand?
{Doubtful.}

No one looking six inches past their noses,
Engulfed in that great "Virtual Cloud" of roses, as
The "Four Horsemen" ride in
{Unopposed.}

The "Machine" prepared the way, and stole our Souls. . .
{And the band plays on.}

Usually, from twilight until dawn
I sit about and write and make songs.
Talk about the places I have been.
Things that I have seen,
People I've known,
The lessons of joy and of sin.

· 'Bout all of the times that
Dreams almost came true, when
There was a value and worth to life.
And about those days when
It seemed like everything, was
Wrapped up in self-inflicted strife.

Take the good and the bad and
Finally realize that
The two are both "partners in crime."
Cannot understand one without the other.
It equals out and makes the poetry rhyme.

To give a reason to this journey
That we find ourselves on, and
Maybe find some like-hearted spirits to share
The awe and the wonder,
The pain of life, and of death.
The "Gift," is when you are able to care.

Be Blessed.

All of these changes
All these things going on
Sometime it's just crazy but
You can always find a song
Let you leave it alone for awhile
Think back on times
That make you smile
When you could play on through and
Not even think about tomorrow

Now that we've all gotten a bit older and
We feel a little colder when
The wind blows in December
Don't you know
And we try not to remember
That everything must pass
Time comes
And every one of us will go
Into the water of Forever
And feel the river flow

So take this time while you have it
Before it goes away
Get some "Treasure Time" in with your
Family and Friends
And do not be afraid to say
I Love You

Peace

I trust my heart and my faith
Fuck everything else
Though it gets almost unbearable at times
If I persevere – The sky eventually clears
And again I can find some piece of mind
Albeit only for a little while

Just have to "Leave it go" every now and then
Get out from beneath this large "Shit Pile"
More commonly known as
The world we live in
We have fucked her up good
Seem like such a sin
And there isn't any going back now

So you wait your turn
Pray hard you have learned
All that you were sent here to find
As I walk the path
My faith is my sword
The conviction I feel is sublime
And there isn't any going back now

The song is all about time – And finding it
'Bout accepting the truth – Not hiding it
Eventually all things merge and become the same
Time to learn to love again while it is still allowed
Throw out all the bullshit and the games
And learn to Love and Share again

On occasion,
In order to love,
You have to hate something else.
To discover,
You have to throw things away.
Find the truth
In a lie,
Become contemplative and sigh, then
Say a prayer, and
Get on with your day.

HooAhh!

A great many people today
Have much more than they need.
Do not give a thought at all to sharing.
Live life only to "Aquire."
With no intent in the slightest of caring for
Anyone, other than themselves.

We are sent here, if you will,
To Learn – To Understand.
Waste is a terrible thing,
Especially of Time.
Which does not tarry for anyone,
Woman, Child, or Man.
Here but for a moment, yet
Those who Truly seek
Will find,

That anything relative to
Selfishness and Greed,
Lends to the demise of
Spirituality.
Which is the very thing one needs
To carry on, to the
Final realization of their
Ultimate Destiny.

Be Blessed.

Driving over the road in a "Large Car,"
Peterbilt "379"
A million miles and then some,
I'm talkin' near and far.

Up mountains and through passes that
Have taken lives and kicked some asses.
Through storms of snow and ice and rain,
All alone in the "sleeper"
Except for your dog and the strain that
Comes with the knowledge that the
Only real home you will ever have (or had) is
Out there, with your trusted dog (and best friend)
"On the Road."

We kept the "Hammer Down" and
I am Blessed and Proud, to have
Run those beautiful, endless miles, with you.

Thank you Dakota.
We will meet again. I know it.
Be Blessed, my Friend. Peace.

Life can be tough.
At times it seems you
Lose track of your focus, of
That "grip" on your dreams.
The older you become
The more you get "mean,"
Start to "nip it in the bud,"
Make those breaks total and clean,
Before it ever has the chance to even start.

Know m'friend, that you are not alone.
Basically, we all travel the same road home.

I know that it scares me, what I am saying, but
In my heart I know as well that
Life is just a short video of sorts, playing in an
Infinite imagination,
Best known as "God."

And there it is, boys and girls.
Be Blessed

A person in front of a computer, or
Walking thru traffic looking into a phone,
Is reminiscent to me of a chimpanzee,
Trying to fit a little round ball into a smaller square hole.

There it is, stupid.

Sometimes I wonder about
"Folk" I have known in the past,
Back when our youth had us "rolling asunder,"
Wine, women, and song,
Dressed to the "nines" and pushing on,
Living to party, pillage, and plunder, and
Just having a really fine time.

Here's to hoping that
They are all doing well,
Still upright and breathing,
Having fun and feeling swell.
Getting all they can before it
Comes time for leaving.

Remembering old friends, and
The joyous "Folly of Youth,"
The "Treasure of Memories"
That you never lose.
Still, just having a really fine time.

On "Politicians"

There's just one little thing
I want to say,
If I have to sail into a "shit storm," it
Would help to know which way
The "wind" is blowing.

Syncopated malevolence,
Hiding behind feigned benevolence,
Attempting to dole out magnanimity and
Bring it all 'round in close enough proximity,
To match up with the sheer bull-shit
That most of you are.

Really silly "Political Game Show" hosts.
There it is, Spanky.

At times it is hard
To find a reason,
A "need" for being here,
Should've been rolled up
Dead and gone long ago,
Outlived my utility.
'Least it feels that way to me, and
I don't "cotton much" to walking backward,
So I don't.

Lived hard and fast, it never lasts, so
You get it while you can,
Memories keep you warm when it is cold, and
Winter always comes,
Nowhere to hide or run,
We all watch and learn, as youth turns into "old."
(If we are lucky, I guess.)

Might we all sit down and attempt to figure
While we still have the time to try, how to
Get back to the truth and nature of a human "being?"
Filled with love, compassion, and a willingness to share,
No longer blind, but actually "seeing,"
The way things really are, before all of it goes away?
While we still have a bit of time?

All in the world that I am trying to do is
Figure out a way to understand you
What it is that makes the difference
Who it is you really are
Why you sometimes lie to me and
Why you go so far
To make me think that we do not matter

Devil's Tower in Wyoming
Montana's Little Big Horn Battlefield
North and South – East and West
Showed you what to me is truly real
The shoreline of the ocean – A mountain in the sky
Yet I hear you say that you will not believe
And it makes me wonder why
When I know in my heart that you do

We all dance with a thing called Destiny
The End – Will finally come to us all
Some will pass on peacefully
Others find a long and endless fall
Into Oblivion

What is – What was – Whatever may come
Going to happen anyway
Pray and try to find it – Truth – While there is time
That is all there is to say

There isn't any place that I want to go
Have seen about everything that I need to see
Boredom and bullshit – Make me a wild man
Then you do not want to be around me

Been a real "hoot" and a hell of a ride
And I thank the Great Father
For allowing me to see
The good and the bad – Different sides of
The very same coin – And
I am grateful – I am humbled
I am so ready – To be free

Bring it on

Everyone is mesmerized
Over such mundane trivialities

Do not think or see a few inches farther
Than the end of their nose

It is all virtual and on the screen
A hypnotic trance
Plain as day yet sight unseen

More and more – Everyday
Our "Humanity" goes

Fallen prey to Technology and
The illusory power of Money

Ever seen a hearse
With a computer and luggage rack – Honey

I'm sayin'

All of the clichés one has ever heard.
All of the music and all of the words.
Are there for the knowledge. To help one along.
Truth can hurt sometime, like a phrase in a song.
There is no denying.

You gather up the pieces and
Take the lessons learned.
Trying hard to leave the battlefields behind you.
But know that deep down,
Those fires still burn, and
Sometimes the power of Truth
Has to remind you.

With a song or a verse, like
"I have never seen a hearse
With a luggage rack."
One thing is certain:
We do not come back.
Be best to find it,
While you are Blessed, with
The Time.

The Nature Lady

Mother Earth, so vulnerable
To Humanity.
Rape and pillage Her daily
With our Insanity.
Treasure it – Do not Trash it.
Avoid the Inevitable Calamity,
Borne of Selfishness and Greed.

If we do not – Pay no mind
Take No Heed,
There will be a price to pay. And
Be Aware – It will be Consummate.

Nature has a unique way of
Telling us that something is wrong, and
At this moment – She is Screaming – And
Those in "Power" who should be listening,
Are not.

The Truth at Hand.
Right Here – Right Now!
Long past time to "Not Understand."
To all the "politico's" the admonishment is:
Shit, or Get Off the Pot!
Now.

Know it is close.
Time is coming – To leave.
Can feel it in my Spirit, and am
Ready to Accept it.
Every Warrior Hopes
A Good Death will find him,
Thus attempts to keep distance
From all that can Affect it,
In any Adverse way.

The Second Eternity
Comes to us all.
The End Here – The Final Day.
Whatever is Required,
Try to "Put Things Right."
There is nothing more to say.

Excepting:
Some things never change.
The Spirit, and Forever.
Accept and Endeavor, to
Put it in Order, while you
Possess the Chance.

A person can only handle
So much Humanity.
Too much of anything,
Good or Bad, can
Drive one to Insanity.
Go from Kind and Reassuring, to
Outright Profanity.

All of us in need of
A bit of Solitary Space in Time.

Find it.
Be Blessed.

No one to talk with.
Do not wish to
Interfere or Bother.
Feel as though all is done.
Time has Come.
A fact of Finality. Accepted with
No Consternation or
Need to Holler.
Knowing it will do
No Good at all.

Wonder at times, how it will feel
To take that "Final Fall."
Is it Conjecture, or
Is it Real?
No way to know 'til one
Does "The Deal."

And so?

Continue, to Push On, with
Diligence to the Cause,
Take Pause, and Ponder.

And So?

The Battle

Simple Fundamentals.
Overtly Complicated Technology.
Theology of Being Real.
Machine Induced "Digital Mythology."

Preparation for when it
Comes the Time, to Die.
Too Much Information, to
Confuse, and Hide the Lie,
Radiating Eminently from within
"The Screen."

Bombs, Guns, Knives?
None of the above.
"Computer"
The Weapon of Means.

No Excuse
Not to have seen it coming.
World — Headlong is
Blindly Running,
Straight into Oblivion,
Again.

Seems like we would Learn.

Oh Well . . .

Time Frame: circa 1985/86

Lady Pamela Rush was exactly that
A "Rush" — Beyond Imagining
An ongoing series of Tsunami size Waves
Different Temperatures — Different Shades
With every degree of Profound Passion
Pure Desire — Ancient Ages Olde

Her beauty shined — And
In the depths of her eyes
Burned a Cosmic Sun
She was Magnificent — And
We did so Rejoice — In
The Lust of our Youth
Together—As One
Over a span of many moons
Beyond Imagining

Though now it has been
At least thirty Seasons of Snow since
My eyes last looked into hers — And
Time takes its Toll — On Everyone
Yet
A Pictured Image Never Ages
Nor do Memories — And
This is the Treasure
I can think back on those days
Of her being Beautiful — And both of us Young
Making Spectacular Magic
Together

I cherish this as I
Journey toward the Sun

Adieu

On
Fear, Greed, Ego.

Fear will fall to compassion.
Greed and Ego will disappear.
When Faith is found for the
Acceptance of Truth,
The message is crystal clear.

It cannot be denied.

There are only two choices regarding
The coming "Alteration of Time."
One – Total Desolation – Beyond Belief.
The Other – Magnificently Sublime.

So:

Listen to the Wind.
Hear the Voices.
Wisdom of the Eternities
Whispering to you.
The Secret of Living? In Faith,
You "Let it all go," and
Rejoice in the Simplicity of
Truth.

It cannot be denied.

I think of things
Feel I really need to tell you
But I just don't know
Our situation isn't getting any better but
I do not want you to go
I love you so — From the depths of my heart
I'll do anything that I have to do
Except live in a lie or act out some part
That isn't me — Not even for you
So please

Chorus -

Talk to me — Tell me pretty woman
Do we just need to leave
Escape the madness for awhile — Together
Find some Serenity

Let's rediscover who and what we are
Both with each other and when we are apart
Find a brand new way to get us "back to it" and
All we have to do is start
Please — No need to go our separate ways — Baby
Together we can make it so "Fine"
We draw strength from each other
We are meant for one another
Let's not waste another moment of time
So please

Chorus -

Talk to me — Tell me pretty woman
Do we just need to leave
Escape the madness for awhile — Together
Find some Serenity

Love and Hate are just different sides of
The same coin that we all carry
Old men out riding Harley Super Glides
While their women lay in wait to parry
With the tennis pro or the golfer guy
To receive instruction on how to "swing"
And I am not talking about racquets and clubs
They are getting that "other thing"

And the Band plays on

World keeps on a'turning
Passions flare up and keep burning
Lessons we keep learning
And on and on and on

Pain – It cuts like broken glass
Things come and go
Some kick your ass
So you grab for the good things
When they come your way
Music is one of them
Which is why we play

Step away from the chaos
Of everyday life
Forget for a moment
All the pain and the strife

Move to the Music
Let it dance with your soul
Let it bring us together
The Young and The Old
To Enjoy – The Gift of a Song

The souls of those I have love for
Though physically no longer in this realm
Still are here – In the sense of abiding in me
Helping greatly to keep my craft – Steady at the helm
As I move along this river known as Life

Mine are the eyes they now see with
The emotions I feel come not always from me
Answers to the deepest questions – Solutions to tasks
Even though I cannot actually see
I bask in the warmth of the presence of their Spirits

I yearn for the time that I reach the River's End
And there on the shoreline awaiting me
Will be all those that I love and who love me the same
Finally we shall be together in the truest sense – And Free
To sail away on the Ocean of Eternity

At Last

I can look up into the sky at times and
In the clouds I see
The faces of those I love so much – Now gone
Looking down from above – Smiling warmly at me
Soothing my soul – Like a passive spring breeze

~

A large stone wall now surrounds my heart and
With but a few exceptions
Nothing is allowed entry – To protect what remains
For it is my perception – That death is not alone
Many things – Good and Bad – Come like a thief in the night

~

Friends and Lovers – Family Deceit
Losing all tolerance for Liars and Thieves
Fools – Always talking it – But
You never see them "walking it"
Knock the dust off your shoes and take leave
Because it is never going to change

~

Sun in my face – Wind whispering their names
Even though they are a long time gone
I yearn so badly to go and join them – But
For now I shall carry on
And wait – For what comes in the night
On Guard – Atop the Wall

I do so cherish my little "Flat"
Everywhere I look – Got my life looking back
I can laugh or cry – At the drop of a hat
'Tis where I can truly be myself
Write songs and make the music at
And find a bit of Peace . . .

There be a "circle of energy" – Runs through here of sorts
Folk outside can hear instruments that are not playing
But there are times that you can "hear" it on the tape as well
Not even going to attempt a retort – And that is all I am saying

Saturday Night Jams
Sunday afternoon "Sessions"
Find the groove and play on through
Everyone is in Possession of
The Spirit of the Song
Find the inner strength to carry on through
The Grace of the Music . . .

I sit here a lot – In my little upstairs "flat"
Got a studio in the living room – No "T V"
Feel like stopping in to play – Maybe write a fine song
Come right on over – Bring it on – You know where I'll be
Finding some Peace of Mind – Making Music at
"Flat Number Fifteen Twenty Three"

I'm Sayin' . . .

Come into this world
So innocent and pure
Unaware of the meaning of
Deceit and of lying
Seems just moments later
You are looking back
Try to see where it went wrong
And realize with irony that
You are dying
And
The simple answer is
You did not believe enough in trying

Right there in front of you all along
You just let it walk on by and now
It is gone

Fini'

Sitting here and wondering
What it is I need to do
To make you aware of how it is
That the choice is up to you

You can attempt to understand it
Move on past the strife
You do not just reprimand the bandit
When they try to steal your life

You take them down

Folk look at me and say
"See what you've done to yourself"
And my reply is forevermore
"Better me than someone else"

Lived many lives and spent some "Jack"
Drove 'round in Ferrari's and Cadillacs
Never regretted a single minute
'Cause when things did go bad — Usually
I had gotten us "in it"

So I wear my scars proudly and
On occasion —Still act a bit "loudly"
Be the first to admit I paid the price for my actions
But — We all have to pay and
I Hope and I Pray
That I depart this life with no regret
Just Satisfaction

Go out Swinging— Hard Core

Just Thinkin'

Wake up in the dead of night
Cannot hide from the Truth
From the Wrong and the Right
Of Living
All the Taking and Giving
That each of us have to do
To "Get By" in this world

~

Attempt to obtain a firm grip on things
Fall into Tune
With a constantly changing pace
Come away from it with
Honor and Integrity
Not in a State of Disgrace

~

Know it has never been easy
Was not looking for that
Cannot truly know Joy without Sadness
But
People treat Others
In such terrible ways – And
We must put an end to
This Madness
While God is still giving us the time
To Put It Right

Methinks the thing I shall miss the most when I depart
Will be the warmth of the Sun upon m'face
I know in a small way it may be selfish but
I do not believe it to be a disgrace
To Remember – To Cherish the Beauty of
Such a Wonderful Thing

Every beginning but one has an ending
Yet not one of us here can truly know
The Final and Ultimate Mystery of the Ages
'Til an Angel of Death comes and we must go

Eventually all things merge and become the same
Life is about finding the strength of Faith to get you through it
It is the one short break between the Eternities you are blessed with
To find out if in Truth you can really do it

So in the time I have left I push on and keep searching
As the weather allows – I make time for the Sun
Transcend and commit it to that final place that we all go
Facing West to Meditate and Pray
Find the Wisdom – To get it Done

Ashes to ashes — Dust to dust
Everything Changes
From Diamonds — To Rust
Nowhere to Run — No place to Hide
Jump on my bad motor-scooter
And Ride

Head off toward tomorrow — But
Tomorrow never comes
All you get is Today
So best "Throw Down and Run"

This life is but one room in
A large Mansion of Many
Best "Grab for the Gusto" while you can
There is No Pity

For those who won't
Yet say they will
But when the time comes don't
And
They never will

No Pity

"Fame"

Fame and Notoriety
Are fleeting
Occur and Depart
All of their own accord
'Tis not something that you chase
You will not win the race
Besides – "Fifteen minutes" – Then
Everyone is "bored"

~

The Gift is the "Riff"
One should realize
Dedication – To Improve
Motivation – To Understand
Then – The Mastery of a given Talent
Will Materialize
"Delusion of Greatness"
No longer in the Plan

~

To close
Back in the day in the Great City of Rome
Behind the Emperor and
His Charioteer – Stood
A Royal Servant – With a palm frond
To fan the King and occasionally
Whisper quietly in his ear
How Fame was Such a Fickle Thing – And
Soon enough would disappear
(As was the servant's duty – Per the King)
This is Wisdom

Guess

It either "Does what it do"
Or it don't
Do not want to hear it will if
It is Bullshit — And
It won't
Call it anything you want to
I'll be sure to let you know — And
It had best be "Good" like
You said it would
Take your money friend
And Go

(If it's not "Chicken What Is" we are "gonna be pissed!" Count on it "Bro.")

Adieu

Everything changes
Constantly moving about
Do what we can
Try to figure it out
Just when we think
We have it down to a science
Chaos enters our life with
New "Rules of Compliance" and
Here we go again

Isn't Life just Grand

When I have "outlived my utility"
I just want to die
Not be a pill and tube infested
Lump of shit – Upon a bed
There are many things
Eat on a man
A hell of a lot worse than Death
When I take my final breath – I want the
Competence and Clarity of Spirit to See
Exactly whom it is or what – That
Will finally come for me
My "Escort" to
The Second Eternity

I do not believe that God can fault a man for that

I can always see their faces and
Hear the words they imparted to me
Before their departure to the other place
Before their Spirits were set free

~

I miss them so – One and All – Yet
In my heart I know I will call
On all of them again – Of this
I have no doubt
Have Faith to know
Love is Eternal
That is what it is all about

~

Love
The Foundation of Being
The Center of the Soul
Forevermore

~

Be Blessed

I do what I do – I am what I am
Stay true to myself
Nothing more than a scam – To try
Living – In someone else's dream

Oh – I think of you – Now and then
Hear you singing songs
You had everything one needed
To pick it up and move along
Into a "State of Being"
Where God intended you to be
Then you just dropped it all and ran away
I pray – 'Twas not because of me

Under colored lights
"On Stage Tonight"
Singing songs and looking fine
An Angel – Sent from Heaven
The band keeping perfect time

You just let it go and went away
I pray – 'Twas not because of me
One final note – Just want to say
I do so hope that you found your dream

Peace

This life should be a
Righteous Search for Peace and Love
Ongoing – Every day
Find the Truth and Acceptance
Commit it to Heart
Before it comes time
To Pass Away

~

Into the Second Eternity – Where
The Lessons learned here
Or Spurned
Determine the course set for you
To sail into Forever

~

Best not Dawdle

Nolo Contendre

People sometime ask me – What it is I do
I myself haven't any idea – Was going to ask you
Get up every morning – Light myself a bowl
Drink a cup or two of coffee – Then I start to roll
~

Let the warmth of the sun remind me
It is good to be alive
Watch the smoke a'rise – Keeps me from "Thinkin' On"
All the bullshit and the "jive"
Going on these days – In the world
~

The silly little games
The lies and the pain
The ongoing rape of Mother Earth
Children giving birth – To more children
Think I'll wrap m'self a "big old fat one" pilgrim
Take my ass on back to the woods
'Least there I can pretend that it is all still good
~

Roam up in the mountains
My head "above the trees"
Hear a voice in the waters of a mountain brook
Brings me to my knees
Sometime though I ask myself
Is there anything else I might do
At Present – Feeling Good is Good Enough
It helps to get me through
~

Defense Rests
~

Adieu

Together
Since Time Began
You and I
We have always been
Good and Steadfast Friends

Went through times we had to be apart
Always had that "special place" in our hearts
For each other – In our Souls – Because
Love never dies
Does not matter how or why
It is there – As it has always been
Be such a sin – To stop believing
So – I won't

You have your space – As I have mine
Our mutual respect allows us that
Always "In the Heart"
No matter the Place or Time
No better place than the Soul
For a Treasure to be at
Then it doesn't go away – Not ever

Since Time Began
We have always been
Good and Steadfast Friends
Together

"Fun and Games"

Age might be okay – But "Old Age" sucks
Knees are so rickety – I waddle like a duck
That's been drinking – Starts one to thinking
It's getting close to "Time to Go"
Don't ask me why – Don't really know

The sun is going to rise – We all have to die
That is "The Deal" – And it's not changing
There is just no rearranging of certain things in life
As one continues "waddling" on down the path
Too damned old to stand up in the shower
Now it has to be a bath – Old Age – Whew
Can you spot me a buck – This is starting to Suck
Out Loud

Liver spots on the head – Wrinkles Abound
Look like the Dead Sea Scrolls – On legs walking 'round
What was I saying – 'Bout three minutes back
Damned if I can remember – Think you could spot me some jack
To fix the fender on the Cadillac – Not the guitar

What are we talkin' 'bout anyway – Pretty day ain't it
Oh – Could I get a ride to the Bar
HooAhh

Old – Is Not Gold

See ya – If I can find my frappin' glasses . . .

(Sometime – The Truth is not funny – But one has to try – Aye?)

144

For every "Good" thing on
The internet that one might find
There are a thousand other "items"
Put there to break down and corrupt the mind
Walking about like zombies
Doo Woppin' – Phone at the nose
Can't see a thing – Missing the Lesson – Completely
Like living in a cartoon show
That has no meaning – Except
To keep people away
From what really matters
The Tower – Is Leaning – If we do not learn
The "Fall" will come – And Shatter
And
There is no "Re-boot"

Put that in your "Smart Phone" – Lame Brain

If one has a problem with dying,
Then evidently – Something is wrong.
'Tis the most natural thing – We all have to leave,
Just as any beautiful song
Has a beginning – A middle – An ending,
A three part measure – Life.
If one "finds the groove" – Keeps the "timing,"
"The Last Verse" will come out alright.

Pass on with some Peace – Into the Night,
And be "Done with it."

Dead – All alone – In Darkness
But darkness is just
The Opposite Side of the Light
When one passes over
A different eye is opened within
Can take a bit of time and practice
To Accept – To get it right

Yet – All the while – Just the same – It is there
Faith
Like a Rock – Sustaining – Patiently waiting
To lead one to the Rainbow Bridge
Push On

Hasn't been too long ago
Sixty seven — Sixty eight
Songs — They had a message
The lyrics shot it to you straight

People started asking why
Felt they had a right to know
Scared those in power — People died
"Democracy" — Upholding the Status Quo

Martin King — Another Kennedy
"National Guard" — Killing students at Kent State
The "Convention" in Chicago
Lot of Blood — Whole lot of Hate
Borne of Empty Promises

It doesn't seem we are ever going to Learn

If there is a way to save
What is left of this World
The Answer — Lies in the Music
If we have any part left of our Soul at all
The Song can lead us back around to it
If we do not — I hate to think about
The things that will soon be coming

Lyrics are from that far away place
Bass line down — Guitar is strumming

It all Revolves — Around the Music
If there is any way left to us at all

Sitting here all by myself
Smoke a bowl – There's nothing else to do
Pen to paper – Write a song
Formulate and Carry On
Try to find a way to see
Just what it is I need to be
Before all of it is gone

You are Born – You live your Life – Then Die
What comes after – One cannot know
Find Hell – In search of Paradise
Mistakes – Are how one grows
Hopefully – Before all of it is gone

Reality – Can trump an Ideal
Often does
But you Carry On

Hopefully

A meager one percent of the population
Owns fifty percent of the world's wealth.

Gained from digital manipulation of
The other ninety nine percent of us.
No thought to our welfare or our health.

Altruism what?

Man believes he is endowed by God
{Or Science}
To rationalize everything.

Which is exactly why it is so fucked up.
Everywhere.

Faith is the key.
Never give up.
Pray and Meditate.
Practice the "Art of Patience."
Do not procrastinate.
Remember that Time is Relative.
Accept that all things must pass.
Exception: The energy of the Spirit,
Moving onward – Forever lasts.
Apathy is a destroyer of all things good.
Doubt kills – Literally.
Ego – Decimates the Soul.
Compassion – Conquers fear.
Do not be judgmental.
Keep those you Love as near,
As you can – And
Press On.
Be Blessed.

Prayer and Meditation
Practice as a Martial Art
Perseverance and Forgiveness
Both – Integral parts

Progress – Not Perfection
Nor Delusions of Grandeur
Discipline of the Spartan
Keep the Spirit – Strong and Pure

Always Ready – For the Coming of
Death
'Tis not until that moment – In that
Last mortal Breath
One is Truly Borne

Eh . . .

Loose Nukes
Biological Plagues
African "bats" – Killing thousands of people
Lies – From the world's "Political Game Show Hosts"
Me'self – Am looking for a steeple
With a church underneath
Fall to my knees – Face the Altar
Pray

If we do not wake up soon
Come to our senses – Get hold of the Truth
It is all going to Pass Away

Killing children – In the name of god
'Tis Blasphemy – Plain and simple
All a maniac understands – All you can do
Put a bullet – Into the bastard's temple

And be done with it

Look into the eyes
    There is frustration
Gaze deeper
    There is the Spirit of Hope
Feign what one must
    To get by in these times
Where falsehood and Truth interlope . . .

Ask the Great Power for Strength
    Every day
To persevere and overcome
    The latent Thievery of the Machine
Chipping away piece by piece
    Our humanity
Pure and unadulterated insanity
    Technology – A Curse, and
The worst remains yet to be seen . . .

It is there in the eyes
    And it is imperative
To once again establish "Balance"
    Put the verses back into rhyme
To become a human "Being" with
    Eyes capable of "Seeing"
To become "Real" again
    While there is time . . .

To inhabit the aloneness of solitude
Marvel at the vastness of it all
Bear witness to the magnitude and realize
Out here one needs no eyes to see
Nor ears to heed the call
The Spiritual
No need for chants or mundane rituals
Allow it to be
Learn

Incoming

Back then
"Back in the day" as they say
A man had to be fast
Quite fast – Both on his feet
And with his mind
To "Get by" – To Survive

Three Canopy Jungle
Tigers and Sappers
They do what they do – And
You do "same same" – Which is
Whatever it takes – To stay alive

To keep up-right
Stay wound up "tight"
"The Bush" – It cuts no slack
Fuck up out here my brother
Make a mistake – You ain't going
To make it back
Except in a tin box – If that
"There it is"
Sin Loi – G. I.

Yeah – Back then
Men seemed more like men
Before we lost our
"Hearts and Minds" to
The bull-shit and propaganda of
"Technology" and "The Machine"

Makes it all so worthwhile – Doesn't it
Fucking Hilarious

Sin Loi – Boys and Girls

The Eternal and Almighty Power
   At times has to work in mysterious ways
To bring one back around to
   The infinite Truth of the Heart.
That the strength of Faith and Spirit are
   Fundamental to survival, and
There is no time like the present for us to start.

To learn to discern,
   Before the whole world cracks up and burns,
We must find and practice
   The discipline of real Love again.
How to give to and care about each other, to
   Realize that all of us are sisters and brothers, and
Get back into what it means, to be "friends."
   And that a "family" that has Love,
Will never end.

Alone by myself
    In the dead of the night
That is when it comes to me
    With the darkness and silence
I can find my thoughts and
    The clarity of purpose to see
The answers to my questions

Life now is just some photographs
    Framed and hanging on the wall
Women, cars, and rock and roll stars
    I really had myself a ball
If I'd the chance to do it over
    I would do it TWICE y'all and
I wouldn't change a thing
    It is who I am
The Truth – The Lie – The Scam
    Said I would not change a thing

I smile in the darkness
    And carry fucking on

If civilization were to fall away
In the blink of a viral plague's eye, and
You were one of the few that made it through,
Would you wish that you had died?

No internet, no "Face-Book" to
Wile away your life, on
Trivial and mundane illusions, whose
Only purpose was to disguise the coming strife,
Cloaked in the confusion of
"Technology."
Would you wish that you had died?

Was it not enough to be thankful
For what we were given?
The Good Earth, clean and pure.
Real Love and Compassion,
Respect for all things,
To strive together, to endure.

Before we allowed technology to
Turn the "Art of Living" into a blasphemy, and as
You wonder how you survived the catastrophe,
Would you wish that you had died?

Not really worried
About "impressions" any longer.
It is enough for me – That I know it.
Vindication for myself
Is not for anybody else – It is all about my soul and
Making it stronger.

Finally came in and got close
From so far away.
At first – Had a bit of trouble seeing.
The truth of it was there
All along – But I didn't care.
Oh – I was "human" but
Hadn't the slightest idea about "being."

Have lived out my life
With very few regrets.
Bad times taught me true appreciation
For the Good.
And if I had to bet – I would wager my soul that
Love has gotten me through it – As
Deep down in my heart
I have always known it would.

(just had my "eyes" closed for a bit)

Ah, Colorado ...

Standing in a mountain stream
Fly-fishing for trout,
Enjoying the proverbial "doobie" and
Not having to worry about
A thing in the world but the enjoyment of the day.

From Trinidad up to the
Red Feather Lakes in
The Roosevelt National Forest,
Antelope, Buffalo, the Eagle, and God,
Truth is apparent both for the rich
And for the poorest, and
For a moment, I put down my creel and rod.

Bring one to their knees.
Open the eyes in a Spiritual Way
To really "See,"
The sheer honesty of the mountains, and
Letting the Soul fly free.

For me, the Pure Simpleness of Truth
In Colorado.

Be Blessed, All ...

The "Wedding of the Rivers"
The Merging of Souls,
Must come to us all,
There's no doubt.
Have some fear, yet you know
That one must be bold, and
Reach to find the Faith
To work it out.

Anymore, I do not
Live to find Justice, nor some
Vain excuse or
Vindication for my life.
I have done what I have done,
Been some bad times, but had more fun, so
"Whiskey – Tango – Foxtrot?"
Not a whole lot more to say.
"Whiskey – Tango – Foxtrot?"
Just living for Today.

Which is in Truth, all that we have.

Be Blessed Always, and
Go in Peace.

Sometimes
A smile helps to hide the pain
Felt down deep inside
As the sun dries up the fallen rain of night
There are times you know
We all need someplace safe to hide
Drop back ten and punt – No wrong – No right
Just need to take a little time – That's all
Take a little time

These days
I do my best to keep my distance from
Most everything but me
At least I still can get along with myself
Up to an extent I am good with everyone else
Then it goes straight to hell in a hand cart and
That's one place that I do not want to be

Smile and Push On

You live and learn
You play – You pay
Life isn't easy – Then you die
Not a whole lot more to say
Run with it – Do not wonder why
Only so many hours in a day and
"Today" is all you have

Be Blessed

Eternity might be no more than the
Eight minutes or so that it takes
For the brain to finally die
Time is such a relative thing you know
There is no telling how it is or why
Until you actually arrive
On that "other side"

Might start in a box with
Two levels of rooms with
A table and book and a chair on each side
You enter and sit down with
An all-seeing entity
There is nowhere to run or to hide

From the Spirits all around
Across the Rainbow Bridge
Wherein all souls abound
In the Second Eternity

Be Blessed and Go in Peace

09 November, 2014

Been twenty five years since
The fall of The Wall
Berlin has yet to become one city
Communism may be gone but
In spirit it lives on
Still more political "hot air"
Such a pity
Some things will never change

Built in nineteen sixty one and
"Endorsed" by border guards with guns
Barbed wire – Blood – and Manifesto's
Of the day
ICBM's with ten megaton heads
Maniacs willing to kill everything dead
Already damned near "did it" several times
What can you say
Some things will never change

Today the missiles are still firing
There are viruses and plagues
"Special Operators" needing hiring to
Keep down the "War Crimes" at
The Hague

Technology – Greed – and Power
The triad that knocked us down
The Wall
Some things never change
Such a pity

Early morning,
  Time again,
To go deep inside myself.
  Try to find the answers
That I seek.
  Bring some peace to
My troubled soul
  Which I so badly need, to
Persevere and get along
  With everybody else.

Taken some "hits,"
  It is part of the game, but
Regret for the past
  Will drive one insane,
If you let it.
  Best to forget it, and
Remember that all you have
  Is "Today."
So treasure it, and
  Take it on down the road.

Carry on, and
  Continue on down the road.

I miss going up into the mountains with my father.
Fishing, drinking, talking.
My father was "of the land," and he loved to fish, as I.

I miss my mother's hugs, and cooking, and
Our conversating together.
She was a Saint.
A pillar of strength and conviction in her beliefs.

I miss my brother.
Our times together were adventure stories.
We had the best of, and the worst of, shared between us.

And my Dakota . . .
We were everywhere, and did everything, together
Twenty-four/Seven.
He was a gift from God, a Holy Spirit who
Taught me to Love and Care again, after those
Feelings had been ripped asunder by
Circumstances that I had no control over.

We are one. Still together, though for now at least,
We dwell on different sides of the same canvas.

I miss them all dearly, but
My Dakota and I . . . There aren't words.

A Dog is just God, coming at you backwards.

Peace - Eternity

Would that we could go back,
    To those times now long ago past.
When everything seemed fresh and new,
    And we all thought that it would last.

When a promise was not given without
    A devout intent to keep, and
The children were the most important thing, and
    The prayer was simply
"Father, Now I lay me – Down to sleep."
    'Twas a blessing just to be here,
Know what I mean?

What happened? – Where did it go?
    Been so long now, I'm damned if I know.
Back when living was an art – Before we
    Allowed "Technology" to start
The fifth and final desecration of humanity.
    "The Machine" is now rendering it's
Digital "Manifest Destiny," and
    We brought it on ourselves . . .
We brought it on ourselves . . .

Oh, I still believe in magic,
Although I know that it's not so,
Except for some
Whom have the "eye" to see, and
Think about that time to come,
The Final Destiny.
The Second of the two Eternities.
The Ultimate of all Reality . . .

Be of very much import
To be in total, focused.
Be done and gone before
The second coming, of the locusts.
And to have found the faith, down deep inside
To have done it right.

Would that when Death comes to me,
It will lift me like the Wind, and
Carry me a million miles away, into
An Infinite and Cosmic Galaxy
Full of little children and animals of
Every kind, at play.

Where Love abounds, and the only
Sounds are soothing.
Rainbows in the Sky, and
Never-ending days.
Just cross the Bridge into Forever, and
Keep on moving,
Toward the Truth that surpasses understanding,
Be Blessed – Welcome Home,
There is nothing more left to say.

"Annudder" one, eh? Wott?

I converse with folks
Through my writing.
My deepest feelings are
Inside of the song.
Music and Prose
Are the life that I chose.
Nobody but me.
I carry on.

The Blues, at times are
Hard to live with, but myself,
I cannot do without.
Writing about the pain and sorrow,
The price we all pay,
Helps me to "get on through" to tomorrow,
Singing "The Blues" Today.

Might even learn a lesson or two.
With the Blues, you never know.
Won't let the door hit me in the ass leaving, but
It is time for me to go.

Adieu.

For Emma and Dave

Love one another
Keep the Faith
It will keep you strong
Together
Persevere and be wise for
This journey you take
If you really want
Can truly last Forever

When two become one and
Love shines as the Sun
Infinite and never ending
Each of you equal
Eye to Eye
and
There is no pretending

Keep the Faith
Trust in the Love
'Tis yours
If you want it

Peace

To err is human
    'Tis a major part of the game
Knowledge acquired through
    Mistakes made moving down the road
Lessons not learned will
    Eventually drive one insane
Awareness of the Truth
    Girds the Spirit
To bear the load

The ones that are best
    Hits one hard — To the chest
Pain of Betrayal — The Anger
    Cuts deep into the Heart
Playing another Soul
    Like a bad violin
Love is Beautiful
    Sometime though
It can only work out
    If those involved — Remain apart

Wisdom would be
    'Tis better to love
Away — From a distance
    Than to lose everything
Due to an impossible insistence
    From someone whom as of yet has
No idea of the meaning of the word

    Be Blessed — Push On - Learn

With the word
There is only the writer
Alone and intensely in focus
With the page
The way the lines fall are
The brush strokes – Like
Paint on a canvas
To Engage

Implore the Mind
To look at Life through
The prism of the Soul and the Heart
In search of something
Lost long ago
Knowing the quicker one starts

Might still have time
A chance
To find it – Once again

Let go for a moment
While there is time . . .

How did all of this happen?
Why did we allow it to transpire?
When was it that we crossed
The point of no return?
Right in front of our eyes,
Those in power gathered to conspire.
Steal what little was left remaining, and
Leave the common man to burn, in
The "fodder" of broken political promises and lies.
The "Chosen Few," they make it through.
The "Masses?" — We just die.

{But mon ami, that has been the "Plan" all along.}

For me
        Writing is like rhythm
In a never ending song
        Words falling as they do
Upon the page
        Every line has its space and time
Like Symbolic Patterns
        From a different Age
So Meaningful – So Real
        It will take your breath away
The Rhythm
        In a never ending song

I love it so . . .

I just have to say it
There is no other way to play it
I am a fool for your loving
But I have to go
Break me down so bad
Going to die if I don't
Pack myself a bag and
Catch m'self a boat and
Sail on out of this shit now
While I can . . . So
Good Bye – Sweet Dreams – Adieu
From this old "Blues Man"
Once again
Good Bye – Sweet Dreams – Adieu
Moving on

If it is coming from the Heart
Let it flow
If the "mind games" cut in and start
Then it is best to let it go
If only for awhile to
Find what it is one needs
And get back to the Truth

That only Love sustains
Flows like a river to
Wash away the sorrow and the pain
That come with Living
Some taking – Others giving

And if that turns into a game
Then it is best
To let it go

For a little while – You know

Be best just to leave it go – For a little while

If I could but sit you down
And tell you, I would.

But then it would not
Be the same anymore.

I can show you by example, but
You must open your eyes to see.

One has to feel it in the heart to
Finally set the Spirit free.

Find that treasured place
With other kindred souls,
Traveling through Eternity.

Together – Forever

Surpasses mortal understanding.
Cannot be ascertained by simple words.

To attempt to merely verbalize it,
Makes it seem outright absurd.

Yet, the simple Truth
Is out there shining,
Bright as the Sun
In a blue crystal sky.

All you have to do to find it, is
Open up your eyes. And see.

Be Free.
Finally.

Side by Side – Different Doors

Parallel Realities
Timeless Mutuality's – With
Each Plane of Existence in Partiality
With what Was – Before
Which Is – And will always Be
Eternally – The Same

Need only to open the "Eye" to see – That
There is no Remuneration – For
The Soul to know Salvation
And

For the eye unable to
Shed a Tear
The Spirit can have no Rainbow
The Book is there – For all to read
Quell the Fear
Take a look – Let it go
Finally

Discover Timeless Mutuality's – In
Parallel Realities
Take Heed – Remember
The Science of Energy – Is that
It goes Forever On
And

Eventually all of it Comes together – And
Merges – Into One

So – Boogie, Children!

Nordic Magic
Viking Runes

The Sun – The Water
The Stars – The Moon
An Oracle – A Key to Life

Lessons of Pain
The Scars of Strife
And

Always an Inherent Yearning
For the Process of Learning
The Truth
While there is time

Nordic Magic
Viking Runes
Sun – Water – Stars – Moon

Receive it
Be Blessed
Push On

Keep it in Focus
Trust the Instinct – The Feel
More so than the "Plan"
As the first thing a plan does is go
"FUBAR" – In Continuity
Leave you standing with
Your "Johnson" in your hand
Every Time

Make it up as I go – Then
Execute
Always works best for me that way
Catch them by surprise
"Not a clue in the world"
Leave them with
Dook Stains in THEIR Britches
That is all I have to say

Except – That it always works for me
Mostly

Bye Bye

Do what you must
As will I
Alone – Walking on this
Fog shrouded night
Love you so much – Yet
When I reach out
To Touch
The tacit fact of the matter is
You are no longer "There"

Something is gone – It doesn't feel right
Not Really
"Oh – Don't be silly" – You sigh
Yet even then – The very tone of your voice
It doth belie
The Simple and outright Truth
That being – That you no longer care

Walking – Alone
A Fog shrouded night
Do what you must
As will I

People in large masses
All over the world
Eyes and Minds – Totally
Focused on The Computer
Losing touch with what it means – To be
Human Beings
Allowing the monster of "Technology"
To Neuter
The very Essence – Of
Who and What we are
"The Machine"
In the Phones – In the Home
In the Car
Seems like none of us can
Do without it
Compassion – Sharing – Caring
"Love"
If it is not "Digital"
No one has any time to think about it
Not any more
The sheer volume of Propaganda
The False Information – The Lie
Coming from
Within the Screen
Yet again allowed – To destroy us
Yet again

Faith is what has
Kept me going
For longer than what was
Supposed to be
I guarantee!
The look in your eye
The Divine gift of Love
The Faith
That allows me to see and
Do it Truly!
Sweet Lord – Please
Don't ever take it from me
Amen.

People come into one's life
From out of nowhere.

At times – You have an immediate
Perception
That you have known them all along.

After but a little while,
Without any kind of warning,
Out and about one sunny morning,
You learn that they are gone.

World keeps right on turning.
One continues to Push On.

Say what you will
I am aware – But
On top of whatever else
That is a published book – By
Yours Truly
Sitting up there on the shelf

The Tree – On the cover
Rendered by my daughter
The two of us together
A Team
Put a mutual work of Art
Upon the Water
The launching of
A Dream

There are things that
Money cannot buy
Love being the ultimate Treasure
Words and Portraits of Life
Go Forever On
Provoking thought and
Bringing Pleasure

As one travels along The Path

I never count on any one thing
To get me through
Exception – The Faith
That it will turn out alright
Usually – When it is done
I am standing – Upright and breathing and
If not – Well what the hell
Didn't get to say "G'night"

We all have to leave
Sooner or later
Do no good to grieve or
Worry about
Whatever's coming – When we're through
Is Coming – Don't you see
Oh – I think about it sometimes
But I don't let it bother me

Bring it on
Bring it on
Sittin' shit-faced in a bar
Singin' Blues Songs

Hooahh

Native American
Lodge Fire – Buffalo – Elk
Peyote
Stars in the Sky
The moon at night
The howl of the Coyote

Big Sky of Montana
Grassy – Rolling – Rocky Hills
Little Big Horn River
The Custer Battlefield

Gets one to thinking – Does it not

The Deer – The Dog – The Drum
Peyote
Stars in the Sky
The Moon at night
The Song – Of the Coyote

Bless us Great Father

Came in and got close
From so far away
At first – Had a bit of trouble seeing
The Truth of it was there
All along – But I didn't care
Oh – I was "human" but
Hadn't the slightest idea
About "being"

True to myself
Or anyone else
Until you master the first
You cannot achieve the other

The lesson here being
That "close" only counts
With horseshoes and hand grenades
My brother

Think about it . . .

No Worry

Death is not going to cheat you from
"The Last Appointment"
There is nothing that can keep you away
Night or Day
Wet or Dry
It is what it is
We all have to die

When the time finally comes – And
It does to us all – Be
Nowhere to hide or to run
Away from the Truth
The "Old Double Deuce"
There's no "I'll be leaving now but
I've sure had fun" – It is Done

The Second Eternity
The Final Forever
Sometimes suicide scares me – But I
Never say Never
Know what I mean
Not but a trivial thing – Anyway
Hell – It's Saturday
I'm goin' out Dancing . . .

Adieu

'Tis a long and lonely trek
En-route to Perdition
Hear the Souls Wailing
Brought down by attrition
Of War and Famine – of Gold and Greed
People killing each other over
Things they did not need

Off in the distance – The toll of the bell
Lets yet another know they are approaching
The Gateway to Hell

Was it worth it
Of no matter now
Welcome home – And
If it is any consolation – You are not alone
Words to ponder here are "Consequent Consternation"
Of no real matter – Not now
But still – You wonder
Why?

What happens when we leave here
Where is it that we go
If anywhere
Is it black and without form
A never-ending void
Or
An infinite Gathering of
Kindred Souls
On a Bridge of Rainbows
Together as One
Basking in the warmth and light of
An Eternal Cosmic Sun
And watching the river flow – Forevermore
Faith Sustains – Be Blessed

Me thinks
'Tis better to love one
Away – From a distance
Than to lose everything
Due to an impossible insistence
Concerning something of no real matter

To allow what is at best
A mere triviality
To undermine and eventually destroy
The beautiful and sweet reality – Of
Caring more for another than one's self
A Treasure

Which is why I choose to keep
A Measure
Of space – Away from you
To cherish Love
To keep it True
Adieu

Artificial Intelligence
Now that's an interesting term
"Manufactured High Tech Elegance"
On some words
Can't (or won't) see past your noses
Ram this one up your ass
Here only to destroy us – Send us all to Hell
To Burn

In our own stupidity
Never went in search of serendipity – Or
Anything that might have stopped it – At all
Just "Talked it Up" and welcomed Doom
With the open arms of fools
Then cried like little children
As we were lined up – At the wall
To take our due

Artificial Intelligence
A contradictive and blasphemous term
We did it to ourselves
We deserve to burn

Aye that

"Dat's Right"

Anymore – I try to tell it
Straight from the heart
That I suffered once – From
Self-centeredness and Greed
Yet one day I finally found that
I didn't really need it
Found the strength through faith
To heed it
Now the Truth – It stands alone as
The only thing I need

We carry the weight of "finding" ourselves
Starts the day that we are born
From Paradise to Hell
Then back again
Promises made – Then broken
Lies that turned out True
Words that should have
Never been spoken
I have been there – As have you

And we continue on
We continue on
Searching – For the Truth
Which is the only thing we need
So join me
Please

Covetous Thoughts
{ Eh? Wott? }

I do so covet – Our short
Time together
Have to say it was
The best I've ever had
No matter – Day or night
Nor what the weather
See you smiling with your eyes
Make me glad
God only knows   {pause}
I miss you really bad

Know that all things
They must pass
That is one reality
When I first beheld your face
My life became a song – And
On my knees – In true humility
I told you of my Love – And
You gave it back in spades
Then you were gone

It is about what it's about and
That will never change
Take exception to that notion
You wind up deranged – And
Blinded to those good times
Best I've ever had
Hope you know – I wish you well and
I miss you – Really bad

Saye Wott?

Say it doesn't mean a thing
Yet it does
Swore out loud it wasn't
When you knew so well
It was
Brought the whole thing
Down in ruin
I will never understand
Were you aware
What were you doing
Now I'm a Blues man
{yes I am}

I loved with all my heart
Tried my best to change "me ways"
Mostly – Did a decent job but
I will admit
I had my "days"
One thing in life I treasured was
The Beauty of our Love
Now it is gone – I carry on
With the help of the Lord
Up Above

Just saying
Miss you so much – And
I just hope you see
You sure 'nough meant
The world to me

That's all y'all

The pain of being Lonely
Can be a formidable thing
Persevere – Shed a Tear – Push On
Times that were had were
Good Ones – Forever
Even now – After such a long time gone

Sometimes think
'Tis just the price to be paid
The "Toll"
For doing what I do
Other times – I know
I made a callous mistake
Got confused – And
Wound up hurting you – And it
Haunts me – To this day

Persevere – Shed a Tear – Push On
A Formidable Thing
Sometime

There is Life
There is Death
And
There is the Rhythm of the Lines
Words falling in Syncopation
Upon the Page
Coming in – From out there somewhere
I write them down – They are not mine
Not really – And the Beautiful thing
Is that they never age

Timeless
The Power of the Written Word

"Boogie Children"
Peace

"Amerika"

America's Propaganda Machine.
Obama's West African Lies.
Defending our Home?
"No, I am on the Phone."
That's why we are all going to Die.

Cannot see the woods – For the forest.
"Technology" got into the act.
Strung the masses out on
Digital Heroin.
Took them down, and
There's no turning back.

"Artificial Intelligence"
Dictating what the "humans" will do
Forgot about "being" and fell to
"The Machine"
Now it is over, for the world, for me, for you.
And rightly so – You know exactly what I mean.
Rightly So.

The Infamous "Lewisville Flat"
(Mobe's Joint)

Had some really fine times
Gathered about this round table
"Knights" if you will – Of
Rock & Roll and "Blooze"
Start sometime during the day
Get completely Blown Away
Sun goin' down – Still be doin' it
When it came back through

Sit about and "Bee Bop"
Vocalists wailin'
With all their Hearts
Drums – Guitars – And Keyboards
Kick it in
Most times – It was alright
More than once – 'Twas Out of Sight!
Couple of Spectacular fine moments
Jammed with a Classical Violin
I'm talkin' Cookin'

Yeah – Had some really good times here at
"McScrotom's Lil' Flat"
All things come and all things go – But for a time
Mobe's Joint
Was where it was at

And – You can't take it back Jack
We Beeze Down
And – If I was a betting man
I'd be bettin' that it comes on back around
Fini

Why can we not just
Leave it alone?
Take care of ourselves,
Let others take care of
Their Own.

Talk about God
Amid Tremendous Acts
Of Brutality.
Nothing but the Sheerest
Of Hatred.
There is.no Honor in killing,
Only Necessity.
Without Devout Respect for Life
For All,
Nothing is Blessed – Or Sacred.

Fanatics are Slaughtering
The Children.
"Civilized Man?" Just talking shit.
All about the "Why" and the "How,"
"Logistics & Such,"
The usual "Smoke Blowing" bit.
Children Dying – Mothers Crying.
Politicians? They keep on with the
Same old "Limpid Lines."
To wit: "Gonna be alright, I Promise y'all,
But these situations can take some time."

Yeah, ever'thing gonna turn out just "Fine!"
BULL SHIT !

* On the Soul *

It has been said
"If God did not exist
Man would invent Him."
M'Self, I choose to believe the
"Created in His Image" part.
Either you do, or you don't,
You will, or you won't.
Some never have a clue when it comes
To matters of the Heart.

Sad, but True.
There is nothing one can do but
Offer up a Prayer, and
Push On.

"Machine Head"

(No one looking past their noses. Paying "Homage" to the Phone.)

Seems like anymore,
No one can do without it.
If it is not "Digital,"
Nobody has time to even
Think about it.
Compassion, Sharing, Caring, Love?
Forget about it.

Been "Programmed" to
No longer give a damn.

The sheer volume of misinformation, the
"Digital Propaganda from the Screen,"
Yet again allowed to Destroy us,
Using our Stupidity as
The Weapon of Means.

Could not see the Forest,
For the Trees.

DAMN!

(Some things Never Change. Et Tu`)

If an individual takes the time to
Truly look and study,
To contemplate in earnest, all
The aspects of this Life.
To accept things as they are, and to
Carry On.
Realize, 'Tis a Blessing one is even here,
Despite the hard times and the strife.
(it goes with "The Deal.")

Sometimes, we make the wrong choices
To get to the right place.
Through mistakes, one learns the lesson, and
There is no disgrace.
So long as one obtains the knowledge of
What it means to
Carry On.
To "get it right" while there is time, 'cause
When your turn comes to leave here,
You are "Gone."

Give it a bit of thought. Eh?

Adieu.

"Are You Talking To Us?"

Band Together – Unify,
Shout it.
Still time – To do something
About it.
Truth is stronger than a lie,
Don't doubt it.
The "Lie?" A "Politician."
The Definition of
"False Words."

Delude the "Majority" with
Empty Promises, while
"The Monied Minority"
Line their pockets with Gold.
Rich; They keep getting "Richer," while
The rest of us keep getting "Olde."

And

Those who should, have not a thing
To Say.
Little remainder of time that
We might "turn it around" is
About to Pass Away.

So

Band Together – Unify – Now!
Shout!
Do Something About It!

The "Constant" of Life

The one constant of Life
Is Death.

From the moment one takes
The first Breath.

Nature's clock starts the Time.
If one has the Faith
They will find
The Lesson.

Learn the Answers to the Questions for
The Final Test, that
Comes to us all.

Do not waste it.

Find the Ultimate Understanding.
Before The Clock
Stops the Time.

Be Blessed.

"Jam?" Screw that.
I am "jammin' all the time."
Let's do some
"Improvisational and Totally Creative."
Invent the "Strokes and Chops"
As we move along.
To really "Throw Down and Boogie,"
You have got to "Go Native," and
Pull it all together
"In the Spirit."
It is then you find the
Secret of the Song.

'Tis the only way I do it now.
If not, well then,
I'm Gone.
"Jam?" Goes on a sandwich.
Adieu.

(if it's not going to be "Spectacular," I would just as soon not. That's right. Eh? Wott?)

The memories
　　Though many moons gone
　　　Still seem like just yesterday,
The thoughts, every emotion, again a reality
　　Hear and feel every word that they say
　　　To finally, truly come to understand
　　　　It takes your breath away ...

Sometimes we imitate others
　　In order to discover ourselves
　　　Glean what we can from previous observations
Make a leap of faith beyond heaven or hell to
　　Profoundly define the truth of salvation
　　　Which is what we are sent here to do ...

All that is requisite
　　To ensure that it lasts
　　　Avoid any fear of the future or
　　　　Useless regret for the past, and
　　　Stay rooted in the presence of now ...

As we all roll on resolutely, toward the finish.

A PHOTOGRAPH

Allowing one to linger at
A specific space in time.
A solitary second.
The history of a moment.
Frozen. Through a Lens.

Joy – Sadness,
Beauty – Madness,
The Truth – The Lie,
The Miracle of Birth,
The Look – As one Dies.

A Visual History of
The ongoing mystery of
LIFE.
Frozen. Through the lens of
A Camera's "Eye."

Treasure.

Drive myself crazy sometimes
Trying to figure out what to do
Tired of living in this funky nursery rhyme
'Cause none of it is true . . .

Now it seems that everything is
One big stinking lie
The masses bow down and
Worship the "Machine"
And when it is finished with it's task
We're all going to die
You say "that's just the way it is," and
That is the very reason why
We don't have the slightest chance, know what I mean? . . .

What happened to people talking, or
Just holding hands and walking, on
A beach, or atop a mountain, two alone
To redefine what matters, to
Do what it is that we do
The only "companionship" most folk have now
Is with their phone . . .

Engulfed in some virtual nursery rhyme, and
Not one tiny little bit of it is true . . .

Oh brother – Do you mind turnin' it down
My ears are really startin' to ring
All a dull roar and I hate to say
It's just a cheap imitation of the real thing

Back in the day – All kinds of music
Really turned the people on
It was new – It was fresh
The blues and rock & roll wrapped up in
Timeless old gospel songs
Ever'body in love with each other and
Nobody could do any wrong

Livin' the high life – Throwin' it down
Having a fine time with the ladies
"Betty White" and the others
Makin' music with the brothers
A sheer joy to be alive every day
When did all that spirit leave us – I got to know
And why did it go away

Now – Every damned thing is "digital"
Computers dictate to the masses
A machine cannot replicate "humanity"
Won't find anything "on line" teaching classes
On brotherhood or morals or fear

I say – Oh brother
Would you mind turnin' it down
My ears are really startin' to ring
I hate to say it but it's my observation
It's just a real cheap imitation of the real thing

214

Am just the hand
That writes it down,
The message is in the words,
That fall the way they do
Onto the page.
Sometimes a Blessing
Can be a curse
Life is for better,
Or far worse.
Seems like nobody
Gives a damn,
Blows me away . . .

While you are young,
Get out and travel,
Learn all the history that you can,
Helps to unravel, the
Falsehoods, from the
Truth and mystery of it all,
Not any way to know for certain
'Til it comes time for you to fall . . .

Like the words do,
Onto the page,
Who knows from where
Or really cares,
I keep hearing myself say
There is a reason, {has to be} to
Keep "pushing on,"
Guess I'll go out on the lake,
Write a Blues Song . . .

Evolutionary Biology.
Brain Sciences – Paleontology.
The Archaeology of Anthropology.
Total Breakdown of the Species, by
"Educated Man."

Draw from the Thesis on
Self-Rationalization.
There's one to Ponder.

Each and every one of us do it
At the Least – Several times a day.
Assists us in putting Fault – Or
The Truth of things at bay.
For those few minutes – 'Til it
Disappears in its Entirety and
Goes Away.

And

With an Unabated and Clear
Conscience – Back on Stage,
We continue with our "Play."

Ah – Speculative Arbitration:
What else is one to say?

Eh? Wott?

Nourish the Youth.
Teach cooperation
Longevity – Soulfulness.
The meaning of One.
The Ability to Reason.
That True Wisdom is
Self-understanding.

That Psychotropic Medication is
Drug induced Alienation that
Closes the Eye of Truth and
Leaves the Soul without
The very thing it needs to
Carry On:
The Realization of Self.

Teach – Be Humble.
The Child is raised by
The Tribe.
By Example.
Be Thankful, and
Nourish the Youth.

Adieu.

All you can do with the past
Is leave it where it is at;
Behind you.

Learn, and Push On.

About the Author

I refuse to apologize for what I am,
For my strengths or absurdities,
If I had it to do again I would not change a thing.
Because all of that,
"The Journey"
Is in and of itself, quite specifically
The reason I am "me" (That's it.)
Be Blessed

Author's Note:

This is the second printing of the second book.
The first, we'll write off as a large misunderstanding. . .
Here's to the concept of correct . . .
(Maybe)
HooAh!